Corporate Governance

Understanding the Board-Management Relationship

H. Stephen Grace, Jr.
Suzanne H. Gilbert
Joseph P. Monteleone
S. Lawrence Prendergast

ABA
AMERICANBARASSOCIATION
Business Law Section

Cover design by Catherine Zaccarine.

Printed in the United States of America.

28 27 26 25 5 4 3 2

ISBN: 978-1-63905-434-3

TABLE OF CONTENTS

PREFACE vii

ACKNOWLEDGMENTS ix

INTRODUCTION 1

I. ECONOMIC FUNDAMENTALS UNDERLYING ORGANIZATION GOVERNANCE 5

A. The Economics of Ownership: Governance, Oversight, and Management 5

B. The Caremark Duties 6

1. The *Marchand* Decision 7
2. The *Boeing* Decision 9
3. McDonald's I 11
4. McDonald's II 13
5. Meta 14
6. What are the takeaways for counsel in all these *Caremark* claims? 15

C. The Evolution of Board Responsibilities within the Context of Personal, Political, and Organization Governance 16

1. Personal Governance 18
2. Political Governance 23
3. Organization Governance 25
4. Board and Board Committees 27

II. STRESS TESTING YOUR ORGANIZATION GOVERNANCE STRUCTURE **29**

A. Stress Testing Governance Structures: An Introduction 29

1. Strategy-Plan-Operate-Control Cycle 29
2. From Tone at the Top to Checks and Balances 31

B. Board Governance: The Fed and Wells Fargo; Blue Bell and Boeing 31

C. Governance's Often Pivotal Role in Litigation 32

D. Putting the Governance Structure Under the Microscope 33

1. Revisiting the Division of Labor 33
2. Stress-testing the Corporate Governance Structure 33
3. The Good, the Bad, and the Ugly 33

III. EVOLVING FROM TONE AT THE TOP TO CHECKS AND BALANCES **37**

A. The Tide Begins to Turn 38

B. Shifting Focus from Tone at the Top 40

C. Paul Volcker and Arthur Levitt on Checks and Balances 42

D. Board Oversight and Governance: From Tone at the Top to Substantive Checks and Balances 44

1. Mandating Improved Board Oversight and Governance —Wells Fargo 45
2. Evolving from Tone at the Top to Checks and Balances 47
3. Effective Governance Includes Ethics, Values, and Corporate Culture 48
4. Improving Oversight and Governance Is Timely and Good Business 50

E. Boeing and the Ongoing Evolution of Director Responsibilities 50

1. In Re The Boeing Company Derivative Litigation, Court of Chancery, State of Delaware, C.A. No. 2019-0907-MTZ, *Decided* September 7, 2021 51
2. Identifying and Addressing Fundamental Governance Breakdowns 51
3. The Economics of Organization Governance 52

IV. WHY A COMPANY SHOULD CONSIDER USING AN EXECUTIVE COMMITTEE OF ITS BOARD OF DIRECTORS 53

A. What is a Board Executive Committee? 54

B. Three Reasons for a Company to Consider the Use of an Executive Committee 55

C. Some Caveats for Creating and Using an Executive Committee 56

V. ORGANIZATION GOVERNANCE AND INFORMATION GAPS: IMPORTANCE OF INTERNAL REPORTING AND INTERNAL INFORMATION FOR BOARD OVERSIGHT 57

A. Introduction 57

B. Quantity of Information—How Much is the Right Amount? Who Decides? 59

C. Quality of Information Supplied to the Board—Issues in Measuring Financial Performance 60

D. Non-GAAP Measures in External Reporting 62

E. Using Internal Reporting Design and Cash Flow Monitoring to Understand and Manage Effectively 63

F. Cash Flow Monitoring—A Key Measure of Performance 63

G. Corporation and Director Obligations for Public Reporting and Disclosure 64

VI. MONITORING CASH FLOWS: THE BOARD, THE CLO, AND THE CFO 67

A. Introduction 67

B. Case Study 68

C. Cash Flow Emphasis: Can't Be Overrated 68

D. Authority for Cash Flow Management and Cash Control 69

E. Analytical Model 69

F. Cash Control Activity 70

G. Liquidity Requirements and Forecasting Difficulties 71

H. Company-wide Cash Flow Reporting Structures 72

I. Cash is King 73

J. Conclusion 73

VII. THE BOARD, MANAGEMENT, AND THE ORGANIZATION'S INTELLECTUAL CAPITAL **75**

A. Examining Personal Governance Systems 76

B. Management and Boards—Responsibility, Accountability, and Service 77

VIII. BOARD MEMBER SELECTION AND BOARD INTERACTION **81**

A. Board Member Selection—Mission Critical 81

B. Board Interaction—Equally Critical 82

IX. CONCLUSION **85**

A. Current issues 85

B. The Ongoing Evolution of Governance Responsibilities 86

Appendix I "The CFO and Public Policy," The Corporate Report—Second Quarter, 1997 **87**

Appendix II Challenges Facing a Centrally Planned Economy: The Grace-Samuelson Exchange, The Quarterly Journal of Economics, May 1970 **101**

Index **105**

About the Authors **109**

PREFACE

In the past few years, there has been a steady stream of headlines on corporate negligence, improper behavior, and questionable decision-making. Scrutiny has fallen on corporate boards and how they have failed to provide adequate corporate governance.

This new book, *Corporate Governance: Understanding the Board-Management Relationship*, provides a candid analysis of corporate management; the legal liability of directors and officers; and, most importantly, how the corporate board has evolved and changed—dramatically. Fortunately, the authors of *Corporate Governance* have the experience, knowledge, and practical understanding which gives the reader a firm grasp of the development of corporate governance and what this means for prosecuting or defending corporation litigation arising from governance issues.

The authors have provided a unique and focused lens in which to evaluate and understand the actions of directors and officers and their implications for corporate executives, legal counsel, business managers, stockholders, and consumers. *Corporate Governance* offers a textured perspective of a complicated subject that is often misunderstood by both professionals and the public.

It was the need for that perspective that led me to engage H.S. Grace when managing the claim for the primary layer of D & O insurance coverage of the Disney derivative litigation over the not-for-cause dismissal of Michael Ovitz, and the resulting no fault termination package he received. The H.S. Grace analysis and insights regarding the soundness of the Disney board's decision regarding the hiring, compensation package, and termination of Michael Ovitz provided the foundational analysis that ultimately led to the decision to litigate—and the result was a total defense victory!

The wisdom and experience of H. Stephen Grace, Suzanne H. Gilbert, Joseph P. Monteleone, and S. Lawrence Prendergast are readily apparent on every page of this compelling book. *Corporate Governance: Understanding the Board-Management Relationship* will be the "go to" source for business and legal professionals as they seek guidance on this important topic.

Dave Gilfillan
Chief Claims Officer, CRC Group

ACKNOWLEDGMENTS

The authors wish to recognize the insights and writings of other members of Grace & Co. Consultancy, particularly that of John E. Haupert, Sheryl Hopkins, and Susan Koski-Grafer. The authors benefited from the thoughtful coordination and fine work of our two paralegals, Allsion Hawkins and Leslie Maxey-Munoz.

To say this book benefited from the involvement of the ABA Content Guy, Rick Paszkiet, is an understatement. His guidance, input and direction was literally continuous and it was a pleasure working with him.

His Team was right there throughout, particularly Caitlin McCauley and Katrina Krause. Likewise, a pleasure working with them.

Finally, the authors thank the ABA members, unknown to us, who served as reviewers, raising thoughtful questions and insights from the origin of the project.

INTRODUCTION

The objective of this book is to present an economics-based legal and business perspective of essential elements of organization governance, which will provide valuable understanding to the business lawyer focusing on corporate governance. This is not intended to be a tome on corporate governance and corporate law, as many other fine works of this general nature are readily available to the practicing lawyer. Rather, we take a unique and practical approach to key corporate governance developments, both legal and in the business arena. The information in this book is essential for the corporate governance lawyer to develop a truly comprehensive, strategic view of organizational responsibilities.

In particular, the legal perspective will focus on the duty of oversight on the part of corporate directors and officers—the so-called *Caremark* duty—rather than present an overview of corporate and securities law pertaining to governance generally. While we focus on practical guidance here, consider *The Oxford Handbook of the Corporation* edited by Thomas Clarke, Justin O'Brien, and Charles O'Kelley (Oxford University Press) for an excellent academic overview of corporate governance and securities issues.

Chapter I begins with a discussion of economic fundamentals and specific legal issues underlying organization governance, topics often left unaddressed. Too little attention has been paid to the economic fundamentals of corporate governance as opposed to a straight legal analysis. Without an understanding of the economic fundamentals, the involved lawyer and its clients are doomed to a less than satisfactory structure and an ineffective defense. The economics of ownership focuses directly on the issues of governance, oversight, and management and the parties responsible for those issues. These issues did not appear in their present form, but are the results of long running trends in personal governance, political governance, and organization governance.

It is critical for any lawyer practicing in this area to understand these economic fundamentals to effectively represent clients—whether they are corporate entities or board members—enmeshed in the type of shareholder and related litigation discussed in this book. Even more important, this understanding is critical to the lawyer in advising those clients before litigation takes place and to implement the optimal legal and governance structures to help avoid or at least mitigate the impact of litigation in the first instance.

To understand the current state of board responsibilities and board—management relationships, one must go back not only decades, but centuries. By doing so, we gain a perspective on the forces driving the evolution of board and board committee responsibilities. Included in the influencers are philosophers, spiritualists, sociologists, psychologists, other social scientists, including perhaps surprisingly, economists. Although many lawyers may wince at the need to trace governance principles from the time of the prophet Isaiah, through the Greek and Roman philosophers, and through the teachings of Mother Teresa, this historical perspective in many disciplines deepens one's understanding of modern-day governance issues.

Turning to the issue of stress testing an organization's governance structure in chapter II, we look at the relationships between the elements that exist in the organization's governance structure, and the effectiveness of those relationships in addressing the fundamental responsibilities of governance, oversight, and management. As elsewhere in this book, reference will be made to key legal precedent, academic works, and business experience.

Specific examinations are undertaken and observations offered regarding organization structures that are epitomized by the well-known mismanagement of events by Wells Fargo, Boeing, and others. Additionally, cases where one or more of the authors have participated are set out as examples of the breakdowns that occurred. These breakdowns reflect the complexity of the issues to be addressed in a properly functioning governance structure and the challenges that can be encountered in attempting to create such a structure. The authors strive to give a fair, balanced interpretation of complicated situations that, fairly or unfairly, cast a pall over these corporate organizations.

Chapter III turns to the issue of the evolution occurring, which we, the authors, feel must occur. That is, in shifting from a governance structure based on tone at the top to a structure based on substantive checks and balances, inclusive of tone at the top. The discussion begins by returning to Arthur Levitt's thoughtful commentary in the late 1990s during the period where he served as chairman of the Securities and Exchange Commission (SEC). The work of five senior executives in addressing this transition follows, and, in turn, this is followed by Paul Volcker and Arthur Levitt further commenting on the importance of checks and balances. In chapter III, we address the issues of tone at the top and checks and balances in some detail. In short summary, tone at the top remains an important factor in corporate governance, but even more important is the implementation of an effective structure of checks and balances. The corporate governance lawyer's contribution is discussed throughout this volume.

A lengthy discussion is set out building on the governance collapse at Wells Fargo Bank and the steps the board of governors of the Federal Reserve took to address what they stated to be the failures of every Wells Fargo board member including the chairman/CEO, and the lead independent director. As is well known, almost all of those directors were removed, but will remain embroiled in the associated litigation for years to come. In this chapter, we try to make the reader clearly see this evolution, and we describe each phase of this evolution in detail. The discussion then focuses on the fact that effective governance does incorporate ethics, values, and an organization culture. Further we prove that effective oversight and governance is timely and good business for organizations. The actions of the board of governors of the Federal Reserve arise in the context of their clearly described responsibilities of financial institution directors; these responsibilities can be seen to flow to directors of other organizations.

Then, the discussion moves to Boeing and the negative findings of the Delaware Chancery Court regarding the board's governance and oversight. The vice chancellor's opinion in the shareholder derivative litigation is thoughtful, thorough, and provides a powerful basis for plaintiffs to pursue the board in the litigation that will continue to be forthcoming relative to the 346 deaths that occurred and other matters. Costs, loss of trust, and other factors are all a part of these corporate debacles.

Chapter IV examines whether a firm should consider putting an executive committee in place, consisting of directors and senior executives. The concept of the committee is set out, its membership, the logic for the committee, and caveats to be considered in creating and using the committee. An effective executive committee can be invaluable to the operation of the firm and in the successful defense of the breach of oversight duty claims discussed in this book. Although these claims can never be avoided, it is important for the lawyer and his or her client to bolster the chances for dismissal or a successful defense at trial. It is the opinion of the authors that no system of effective corporate governance will eliminate the occasions for a lawsuit completely. The corporate organization and board can only maximize its chances for a successful defense through implementation and enforcement of these practical suggestions.

Chapter V focuses on information gaps often facing boards and board committees. The importance of internal reporting and accessing certain internal information for board oversight is examined. Both the quantity and quality of information are discussed, the usefulness of non-GAAP measures and the associated care to be taken using non-GAAP measures are reviewed. The critical role of cash flow monitoring is set out, and the organization and director obligation for external/public reporting and disclosure are examined as is the role of the corporate governance lawyer.

Chapter VI drills into the monitoring of cash flows, the responsibilities of the board, the CLO, the CFO, and others for doing so, which are complex and continuing to grow. The collapse of three banks in early 2023, occurring concurrently with the Federal Reserve's sharp rise in interest rates highlighted the vulnerability of financial institutions to liquidity crises. The Federal Reserve website sets out a board's responsibility to create and enforce prudent policies and practices:

"Directors are placed in a position of trust by the bank's shareholders, and both statutes and common law place responsibility for the affairs of a bank firmly and squarely on the board of directors." A board cannot delegate its responsibility for unsound policies and practices. The roles of the board, the CLO and the CFO must incorporate the appropriate checks and balances required by this organization.

Chapter VII addresses an organization's intellectual capital, and the requirements for board and management action and interaction regarding the personal governance systems of today's professionals who comprise an organization's intellectual capital. The expectation is for boards and management to demonstrate a sense of responsibility and a willingness to be accountable and an attitude of service. Inherent in this discussion is the issue of who runs the business, the organization, the school or whatever. Again, we will explore the legal, economic, and business underpinnings of these governance issues.

Chapter VIII turns to the issues of board member selection and board interactions, literally mission critical activities. The complexities of steering an organization forward to accomplish its mission, satisfy shareholders, and achieve related objectives require board members informed, properly involved, and with skin in the game; members who understand their responsibilities, are accountable in addressing these responsibilities, and who bring an attitude of service. Contrasting examples of board member qualification and involvement are examined, both within and outside of board related litigation. We expand on this further in this chapter.

Chapter IX looks ahead, as we review current issues, including those related to ESG investing, and looks at the ongoing evolution of governance responsibilities. Although ESG issues remain a source of some controversy, our focus here is on the G component, i.e., corporate governance rather than environmental and social components that have attracted the most controversy. Future paths for the evolution from tone at the top to governance structures built on checks and balances, the role of the corporate governance lawyer, and the issue of board composition will continue to be addressed.

I. Economic Fundamentals Underlying Organization Governance

A. The Economics of Ownership: Governance, Oversight, and Management

At the outset, it should be noted and emphasized that none of the recommendations set forth in this book, whether individually or in total, can eliminate the risk of litigation against board members and officers. Rather, we believe that implementation of these recommendations can certainly *mitigate* the risks of successful shareholder actions and other suits alleging non-compliance with applicable law.

Also, these recommendations should help the board and executive management better meet the expectations of shareholders and other stakeholders in the corporation.

The economics of organization governance point to the responsibilities of the owners and the agents of the owners for the governance, oversight, and management of the organization. For example, the simple model of a new business started by a single individual who provides the required financing from the individual's personal holdings. That individual is responsible for the governance, oversight, and management of the organization. Increase the individuals to two, three, or more owners, and the responsibilities of these owners and/or their agents encompass governance, oversight, and management.

When there are many owners with various ownership interests, a selection or election of agents may occur. These chosen agents bear the responsibility for governance, for oversight, and for management.

The failure to recognize and properly address these responsibilities constitutes a fundamental cause of the collapses (operational, financial, legal, or otherwise) experienced by a broad range of organizations including large, widely known, for profit and not-for-profit organizations. Examining these organization collapses under a deeply experienced, business-focused lens has confirmed a primary source of these failures to lie in the addressing of fundamental governance, oversight, and management responsibilities (Figure 1).

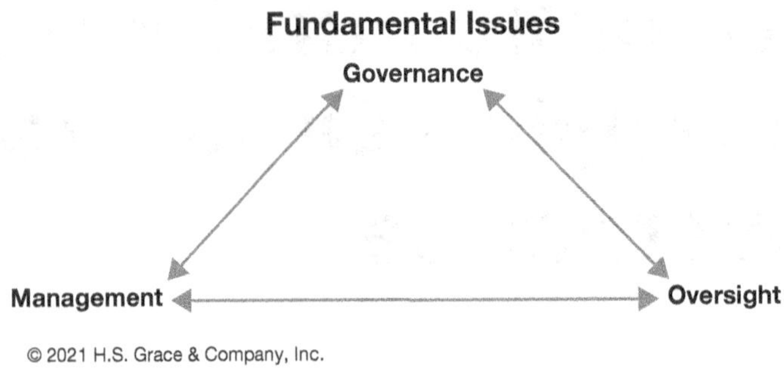

Figure 1

While the organization form discussed here is primarily corporate, the issues and responsibilities apply across all organization forms.

Let's explore a board's duty with respect to oversight and other governance-related issues.

B. The Caremark Duties

A board's duty of oversight over the affairs of the corporation was first well-articulated in the landmark Delaware Chancery Court case, *In re Caremark Int'l Inc. Deriv. Litig.*, 698 A.2d 959 (Del Ch. 1996).

Caremark remains good law in Delaware and is a highly influential decision regarding corporate governance in other jurisdictions as well. The essence of the *Caremark* holding is that a board's failure to attempt to assure a reasonable information and reporting system is an act of bad faith and in breach of the duty of loyalty.

Caremark was the seminal case establishing the conditions for director oversight liability under Delaware law. The *Caremark* test imposes liability on two bases where (1) directors utterly failed to implement any reporting or information system or controls; or (2) even having implemented such a system or controls, consciously failed to monitor, or oversee its operations thus disabling themselves from being informed of risks or problems requiring their attention.

In the years since *Caremark* was decided, the Delaware courts have emphasized repeatedly that claims for breach of the duty of loyalty premised on lack of oversight are exceedingly difficult for the aggrieved shareholders to plead. To state a *Caremark* claim, a plaintiff must plead with particularity that the board cannot be entrusted with the claim because many of the directors may be liable for oversight failures, which is extremely difficult to do. In fact, Delaware jurisprudence suggests that the claim that corporate fiduciaries have breached their duties to stockholders by failing to monitor corporate affairs is possibly the most difficult theory in corporation law upon which a plaintiff might hope to win a judgment. As a result, until the significant cases discussed following, oversight claims have been few and far between and, when such claims were brought, they rarely survived motions to dismiss.

Although *Caremark* remains good and precedential law in Delaware, there have been significant developments in recent years serving to inform corporations and their boards about the perils of becoming complacent in their oversight practices.

Why do some boards become so complacent?

In some cases, the blame may fall on counsel who may unduly stress the improbability of a successful *Caremark* claim. This, however, would be poor legal advice considering the decisions discussed in this chapter.

In other cases, boards may become complacent because they focus only on issues such as enhancing revenue and profitability. Again, the decisions discussed below should curb this complacency by focusing a board on the mission critical activities of a corporation.

It is the role of counsel—both in-house and outside lawyers—to ensure that the board does not become complacent and instead be proactive in responding to the guidance that the Delaware courts have now provided.

1. The *Marchand* Decision

The first wake-up call after *Caremark* came with the Delaware Supreme Court decision in 2019 in *Marchand v. Barnhill*, 212 A.3d 805 (Del. 2019).

Marchand arose from shareholder litigation involving Blue Bell Creameries USA, Inc. (Blue Bell), a Texas-based ice cream manufacturer with an avid consumer following that suffered a listeria outbreak. Three customers who consumed the ice cream died and the company had to shut down production at all its plants. One-third of the workforce was laid off during the shutdown, and a private equity investment was necessary to deal with liquidity concerns. This investment diluted shareholder value.

While the board prevailed in defense of the derivative suit at the Chancery Court level, on appeal the Delaware Supreme Court, applying *Caremark*, found that the board failed to implement reasonable monitoring and reporting systems on mission critical issues. The specific mission critical area of concern was food safety, a key area for any food manufacturer or distributor.

It is important to note, *Marchand* did not change Delaware law; it merely reaffirmed the principles first set forth in *Caremark*. *Marchand* made clear, however, that directors have a duty of oversight for mission critical issues. Directors must implement monitoring and reporting systems to address mission critical risks and their activities must be clearly documented.

Marchand also provided a few important practical lessons.

First, if you are in the food business, food safety should be a mission critical concern. Interestingly, the Blue Bell board had no committee responsible for food safety.

Second, *Marchand* never proceeded to trial after the Supreme Court reversal of the Chancery decision. Instead, the derivative suit ultimately settled for $60,000,000 in April 2020. This was a large derivative settlement that caught the attention of the securities litigation and directors and officers (D&O) insurance communities, although the terms were confidential, so we do not know whether, or to what extent, insurance proceeds may have funded the settlement.

Although D&O insurance typically would provide coverage to board members for these derivative lawsuits, it is not known whether or to what extent Blue Bell may have had D&O insurance in place. Interestingly, in recent litigation brought by Blue Bell and its directors against Blue Bell's general liability insurers, a Texas court held that there was no coverage available under such policies due to the intentional conduct at issue in the underlying litigation and that the policies' requirement for bodily injury was not triggered. *Discover Property & Cas. Co. v. Blue Bell Creameries USA, Inc.*, U.S. District Court for the Western District of Texas, Case No. 21-cv-00487 (order filed August 22, 2022). This decision was affirmed by the Fifth Circuit on appeal on July 11, 2023. No. 22-560842. These insurance decisions were not surprising because shareholder derivative litigation typically triggers only D&O policies and no other types of business liability insurance.

These types of claims remain difficult for plaintiffs to withstand motions to dismiss under Caremark standards. The business judgment rule should remain a powerful defense if the suits are ultimately tried.

The business judgment rule is a long-established rule in corporate jurisprudence that provides a defense for directors against non-meritorious allegations regarding the discharge of their duties. The rule creates a presumption that boards have acted in good faith and within the standards of loyalty, prudence, and care directors owe to the corporate shareholders. Absent evidence that the board has violated the rule blatantly, a court should uphold the conduct of the board with respect to the decisions at issue.

The business judgment rule was perhaps best articulated judicially by the Delaware Supreme Court in *Grobow v. Perot*, 539 A.2d 180 (Del. 1988). That decision set forth five requirements for director acts to satisfy the rule, as follows:

1. The act(s) must have been undertaken in good faith.
2. The acts must have been undertaken in the best interests of the corporation.
3. The acts must have been undertaken by the directors on an informed basis.
4. The acts must not be ones of corporate waste.
5. The acts must not involve self-interest on the part of the directors in breach of their duty of loyalty to the corporation.

It is important to note, the rule protects from liability the affirmative acts of a board. What it does not protect, however, are failures to act, particularly the utter failures to act articulated in *Caremark*.

The key to a successful business judgment rule defense, however, would be that a board level system of monitoring and reporting is in place and enforced. This is an area where it becomes critical that a board receives solid legal counsel. As with the issue of complacency over *Caremark* oversight duties discussed previously, it is important not to overly rely upon the business judgment rule as an automatic defense.

2. The *Boeing* Decision[1]

The second and arguably louder wakeup call came late in 2021 in *In re Boeing Company Derivative Litigation*, 2021 WL 4059934 (Del. Ch. September 7, 2021).

The tragic underlying facts in *Boeing* received much media attention. Boeing manufactured the 737 Max aircraft, which was involved in fatal crashes in commercial flights in October 2018 and March 2019. Various investigations established that Boeing was at fault for the aircraft design and operation. Boeing was sued civilly and criminally and paid more than $2.5 billion in penalties and other compensation.

A shareholder derivative suit followed in Delaware Chancery Court, asserting claims similar to those in the earlier *Marchand* litigation. The Boeing court declined to dismiss the derivative suit and reiterated the *Caremark* standards and *Marchand* ruling by the Delaware Supreme Court.

The Boeing court held that board oversight for mission critical issues must be "rigorously exercised." The court also noted that the *Boeing* board's interest in safety was only passive, as opposed to its much more proactive and vigorous consideration of issues concerning profitability and efficiency.

[1] The Boeing Company's travails have continued after the Delaware Chancery decision and subsequent derivative settlement discussed in this section. In early 2023, a U.S. District Court judge in the Northern District of Illinois issued an order that would allow the relatives of the two 737 Max crashes in 2018 and 2019 to seek compensation for pain and suffering. This order and other litigation brought by the Department of Justice could result in hundreds of millions of dollars in exposure to Boeing. The authors are not privy to information as to what extent Boeing's liability insurance may cover these claims by the relatives of crash victims. Nor are we privy to the scope of release that Boeing and its board obtained upon settling the shareholder derivative litigation. It may well be the case that these potential exposures were accounted for and released in the derivative settlement.

Even more recently there has arisen an incident with a different version of the 737 aircraft involving the failure of a door plug on the fuselage of the aircraft. Fortunately, there were no serious injuries to passengers on board. Boeing has accepted responsibility for the failure. It would be, however, speculative at this juncture to opine on whether renewed derivative litigation against the Boeing board may ensue. Nonetheless, there has already been filed a securities suit seeking class action status. *State of Rhode Island Office of the General Treasurer vb. Boeing Co., et al,* United States District Court for the Eastern District of Virginia, No. 24-00151. The plaintiff alleges that this latest incident demonstrates that the company continues to emphasize profit over safety. Although no independent directors have been named as defendants, Boeing's current and former CEO and current and former CFO are named defendants. As we discuss below in the text, these allegations suggest that the same wrongdoing that so concerned Vice Chancellor Zurn in her ruling denying the Boeing directors' motion to dismiss the derivative suit against them may continue to exist within the company and possibly at the board level.

In particular, the board did not require management to deliver regular safety reports, and management tended to provide only favorable information when it did report.

As in *Marchand*, this decision did not change the *Caremark* standard, but it is a reminder that passive oversight will not do with respect to mission critical issues. While still difficult to overcome a motion to dismiss, the Delaware courts are more likely to sustain a well-pled oversight claim on mission critical issues.

Both *Boeing* and *Marchand* are relatively rare examples of an oversight claim surviving a motion to dismiss. Recent studies, however, have shown that five of seventeen *Caremark* claims have survived a motion to dismiss over the past twenty-five years—an almost 30 percent success rate, against a 70 percent rate of dismissal on the pleadings. Thus, the rarity of these actions surviving a motion to dismiss is legitimately open to debate.

However, an example of a successful motion to dismiss in derivative litigation involving *Caremark* claims would be that in *Construction Industry Laborers' Pension Fund v. Bingle*, No. CV 2021-0940-SG (Del. Ch., Decided September 6, 2022) and sometimes known as the SolarWinds case. In that case, hackers accessed confidential information of SolarWinds's customers. SolarWinds was a Texas software developer, and its customers were various businesses that engaged it to manage their information technology needs. The hack caused tremendous damages to the company's customers.

The shareholders alleged that the company's stock price subsequently plummeted, and revenue was impacted negatively. Further, it was alleged that the board did not have adequate oversight of cybersecurity risk, which was a mission critical concern for this online service provider.

The court noted the proliferation of oversight failure claims, but also noted that simple negligence would not give rise to director liability. Specifically, the court held that "the lack of oversight pled must be so extreme that it represents a breach of the duty of loyalty" and specific pleading of "*scienter,*" demonstrating bad faith. Notably, the court indicated that there were two board committees in place with oversight responsibility for cybersecurity. Although the court found "subpar" reporting from these committees to the full board, this did not constitute an "utter failure" in oversight that would be necessary to sustain a *Caremark* claim.

Bingle/SolarWinds stands in marked contrast to *Marchand* and *Boeing*, at least with regard to ultimate outcome, and it underscores the difficulty that plaintiffs still face in bringing a successful *Caremark* claim. Essentially, the court found that while the board's discharge of its oversight duties was not ideal, it was nonetheless not sufficient to constitute bad faith that would result in liability.

Notwithstanding the win by the SolarWinds directors, one cannot underemphasize the fact that the litigation as typical was costly and the competence of the board was called into question in the eyes of the investor community.

Now, back to the *Boeing* saga.

Shortly after the Delaware Chancery decision, the *Boeing* litigation settled for $237,500,000. While the $60 million settlement in *Marchand* was significant, the *Boeing* settlement was a real bell ringer, constituting one of the largest derivative settlements in history.

There is one hard, practical lesson to be learned from these cases, which is you can never prevent this type of litigation completely. That said, steps can be taken to help better defend against these suits, including successfully moving to dismiss, reducing settlement values even after an unsuccessful motion to dismiss, and perhaps even a successful defense at trial if necessary.

As we discuss further, it is critical to have the right systems in place and to vigorously apply and document them.

Another piece of practical advice is for corporations and their boards to partner with their D&O insurers. This is especially true during hard insurance market conditions, meaning that premiums are high, policy terms may be more restrictive, and insurers can be more selective in choosing what risks to accept. Insurers have become increasingly concerned with ESG (environmental, social, and governance issues) and will look more closely at these potential governance risks at the underwriting stage.

Although ESG investing has come under attack over the years, those attacks and criticisms have centered on the environmental and social components. Governance issues have been of longer-term concerns going back to *Caremark* and even earlier.

It would behoove both brokers and organizations seeking coverage to engage expert consultants, to ensure not only that the best practices are in place and enforced, but also that the corporation is presented to its potential insurers in a more favorable light.

Two significant decisions and one new derivative suit filed in Delaware Chancery Court regarding *Caremark* oversight duties of directors and officers followed on the heels of *Marchand* and *Boeing*. The ramifications of these developments for corporations, directors and officers, and company counsel merit consideration.

3. McDonald's I

On January 26, 2023, Vice Chancellor J. Travis Laster of the Delaware Chancery Court issued a lengthy Opinion in *In Re McDonald's Corporation Stockholder Derivative Litigation*, C.A. No. 2021-0324 (Del. Ch. Jan. 26, 2023) (*McDonald's I*).

The decision was most significant because it extended the fiduciary duty of oversight to corporate officers under applicable Delaware law. As discussed previously, through the court's decision in *In re Caremark Int'l Inc. Derivative Litigation*, 698 A. 2d 959 (Del. Ch. 1996), that duty was one only imposed on corporate directors.

McDonald's I was a shareholder derivative suit brought against company directors, the former CEO, and the former Chief People Officer, David Fairhurst. The opinion addressed solely the claims against Fairhurst in deciding a motion to dismiss brought by him.

In summary, the oversight claims against him were based upon his failure to manage pervasive sexual harassment issues at the company and the fact that he personally also engaged in such harassment of employees on several occasions. Ultimately, Fairhurst and the former CEO, Stephen J. Easterbrook, were terminated separately in 2019 over the conduct at issue here.

McDonald's I caused quite a stir in both the areas of corporate governance and the D&O insurance community, as those insurers ultimately will bear the financial brunt of any increased frequency of these oversight claims.

A careful reading of the opinion, however, indicates that it was quite fact specific and not an altogether surprising result. Indeed, it is not likely that any other officer in the company, except possibly the CEO, could have been tagged with *Caremark* liability for the sexual harassment allegations at issue here.

Fairhurst brought his motion to dismiss essentially on the basis that *Caremark* duties do not extend to corporate officers. The court made clear that officers owe the same fiduciary duty of oversight as do directors "as to matters within their areas of responsibility." As such, it makes eminent sense that Fairhurst would owe these oversight duties with regard to matters such as sexual harassment because that was clearly within his area of responsibility as Chief People Officer of the company. In that sense, an officer's duty of oversight is more limited than that imposed on directors.

The court held that officers had a duty to monitor "red flags" within their area of responsibility and report to their superiors when such red flags are noted. Interestingly, in this case Fairhurst's superior would be the CEO Easterbrook, who was allegedly also enmeshed in the same harassment scenarios. The court noted that a CEO would have a "company-wide remit," but did not further address Easterbrook's liability.

Based on the court's reasoning, it is unlikely that oversight claims could be sustained against Fairhurst if the area were food safety as in *Marchand v. Barnhill*, 212 A.3d 805 (Del. 2019), which we also discussed previously. That decision focused on mission critical areas such as food safety in a company that was an ice cream manufacturer and distributor. No similar mission critical analysis took place in *McDonald's I*, but the court instead focused on the red flag issues.

The court also noted that liability should only attach to directors or officers in these situations if they acted in bad faith and breached their duty of loyalty to the company. In this case, the court held that Fairhurst's own acts of sexual harassment constituted bad faith and a breach of the duty of loyalty.

Many commentators, including those in the D&O insurance community, expressed concern that *McDonald's I* may lead to a plethora of employment law claims being "repackaged" by shareholders as *Caremark* claims and brought in Delaware Chancery. Those concerns may not prove to be well-founded because the facts in *McDonald's I* were particularly egregious. Ordinarily, these claims would not involve misconduct at the officer level and would be directed solely against the company, which in derivative litigation is only a nominal defendant. Based on the reasoning of the court, the claims at issue here could likely only withstand dismissal as to an officer such as Fairhurst who had responsibility for human resources and employment matters.

While other Delaware courts and commentators have observed how difficult it is for shareholder plaintiffs to successfully plead a *Caremark* claim, the court here made no reiteration of this supposed truism. That may be because with this decision and earlier decisions in *Marchand* and *Boeing*, successful *Caremark* claims may no longer be such rare occurences.

As far as D&O insurer concerns about possible increased litigation frequency or opening floodgates in this area, adding officers as potential defendants in these types of claims may have a significant impact on insurers' defense expense exposure. It is duly noted that in *McDonald's I* separate counsel represented Fairhurst and Easterbrook, in addition to the counsel that represented the director defendants. That makes for three defense firms, where normally there would only be a single firm representing the directors and one representing the nominal defendant corporation. In derivative litigation this can result in significatly more (perhaps triple the amount) defense costs liability to the insurer.

4. McDonald's II

On March 1, 2023, Vice Chancellor Laster issued another lengthy opinion in *In Re McDonald's Corporation Stockholder Derivative Litigation*, C.A. No. 2021-0324 (Del. Ch. Mar.1, 2023) (*McDonald's II*).

McDonald's I addressed *Caremark* liability for an officer and was not addressed in *McDonald's II* and thus *McDonald's I* remains good Delaware law with respect to officer liability. *McDonald's II* addressed solely the issue of director liability for the same type of claims.

In *McDonald's II*, the court held that the pled allegations of breach of the duty of oversight against the directors were insufficient to withstand a motion to dismiss. The court also noted this type of red flag oversight claim did not warrant the mission critical analysis undertaken in the *Marchand* and *Boeing* decisions.

Indeed, in *McDonald's II*, the court reached back before *Caremark* to the 1963 Delaware Supreme Court decision in *Graham v. Allis-Chalmers Manufacturing Co.*, 188 A. 2d 125 (Del. 1963) and exonerated the directors from liability under the red flags analysis set forth in that decision. In dismissing the claims against the directors based on the same underlying facts that sustained the claims against the officer in *McDonald's I*, the court reinforced the common wisdom, somewhat eroded by *Marchand* and *Boeing*, that it is difficult to plead a breach of the duty of oversight claim successfully, at least against directors.

Applying a red flags analysis, the court nonetheless held that the business judgment rule provided directors with a solid defense in their decision-making. Thus, despite the fact that the McDonald's board should have been aware of numerous red flags, the business judgment rule protected the decisions they made in dealing with both Fairhurst and Easterbrook. While there may have been in the view of some less than an ideal response to the sexual harassment problems within the company, it was nonetheless a reasoned response protected by the business judgment of the board.

In a real sense, *McDonald's II* relevels the playing field so that successful *Caremark* claims against boards may continue to be rare events.

5. Meta

On March 20, 2023, shareholders in Meta Platforms, Inc. filed a detailed derivative complaint just under 200 pages in Delaware Chancery in *Employees' Retirement System of the State of Rhode Island, et al. vs. Mark Zuckerberg, et al.*, C.A. No. 2023-0304 (Del. Ch. Mar. 20, 2023) (*Meta*). Interestingly, this suit was also before Vice Chancellor Laster.

Meta is a classic example of a breach of the duty of oversight claim and names both officers and directors of the company as defendants. Essentially, the allegations are that Facebook and the other social media sites the company hosts were being used to facilitate sex and other human trafficking. It is alleged the board and executive officers blatantly ignored the problem and failed to act. Among the officer defendants is Meta's general counsel.

As expected, the defendants filed motions to dismiss. On May 10, 2023, in an unwritten ruling from the bench, the vice chancellor denied the motions to dismiss—rejecting defense arguments that the complaint should be dismissed because the plaintiffs did not first demand that the board, as a whole, take action against certain officers and directors. Under Delaware law, shareholders must make such a demand or demonstrate that doing so would be futile because most directors were self-interested, lacked independence, or faced a substantial likelihood of liability.

The vice chancellor noted he was required to accept the allegations in the complaint, which he described as "encyclopedic and specific" as true for purposes of ruling on the motion.

Given that it is an unwritten ruling, this has little to no precedential value. However, in his delivery of the ruling, the vice chancellor gave some indication of how he viewed the severity of the allegations made.

> "[The Complaint] tells a story of directors who were on notice of the law breaking, and who either affirmatively went along with it or consciously disregarded it. What we don't have is a little lawbreaking, what we don't have is isolated lawbreaking, what we don't have are immaterial violations. . . . This is a case involving alleged wrongdoing on a truly colossal scale."

One can only speculate as to further activity in Meta, including but not limited to an appeal to the Delaware Supreme Court or renewed motion practice.

6. What are the takeaways for counsel in all these *Caremark* claims?

The first caveat for company counsel is not to lose sight of who your client is. Simply put, your one and only client is the corporation. It is not the CEO or any other officer or employee; and it is not the board of directors or any individual director. Counsel becomes conflicted when they treat an individual or group of individuals other than the company as a client.

Second, counsel must be cognizant of any provisions in the company's charter or by-laws that may exculpate directors from liability in certain situations. For a long time, these exculpatory provisions protected directors and only in 2022 were those provisions extended to officers. In *McDonald's II*, the vice chancellor took note of such a provision as another reason to support a dismissal as to the directors. This exculpatory provision first adopted in 1986 as Section 102(b)(7) of the Delaware General Corporate Law authorizes a corporation to provide in its charter or by-laws an exculpation of its directors from personal liability for monetary damages in connection with breaches of their fiduciary duty of care.

These derivative suits are often preceded by a books and records demand under Delaware Corporation Code § 220 or similar statute where the state of incorporation is other than Delaware. In *Meta*, plaintiffs have alleged that the company failed to make a complete production of records in response to the § 220 demand. While we have not yet seen the company's defense, it is important that counsel take these demands seriously and not be cavalier in their response. Section 220 demands are not always covered under D&O policies, so consideration must be given to securing an insurance broker's advice as to whether such coverage can be added to the policy if not already there.

Finally, it should not be lost on counsel that Meta's general counsel is a named defendant in this suit. As such, *McDonald's I* may be quite pertinent as to potential liability as a corporate officer. As a corporate officer, the general counsel should enjoy coverage under the company's D&O policy. However, other non-officer lawyers in the legal department would not necessarily have insurance coverage if they were named as defendants in a lawsuit. Although it is rare to have non-officers included as defendants, consideration should be given to procuring an insurance policy specifically designed to cover in-house lawyers for claims.

C. The Evolution of Board Responsibilities Within the Context of Personal, Political, and Organization Governance

Boards and board committees are key participants in the organization governance process, along with senior management (Figure 2). We turn to the evolution of the board and board committee responsibilities.

It is widely acknowledged that an evolution is occurring regarding the roles and responsibilities of boards and board committees. This change in the perceived role has led to penetrating questions regarding the selection of board members, the structure of board and board committee operations, and the board's interrelationships with senior management, the corporate governance lawyer, and the other participants in the organization governance process.

The lawyer must be cognizant of this evolution although his or her sole client is the corporation. In fact, where this evolution creates conflicts in interest, it is incumbent upon the corporation's lawyer to advise the board and/or executive management as appropriate that they may need to engage their own separate counsel.

The Organization Governance Structure

The Structure and Functioning of the Board and Management within Strategy – Plan – Operate – Control Cycle of the Firm

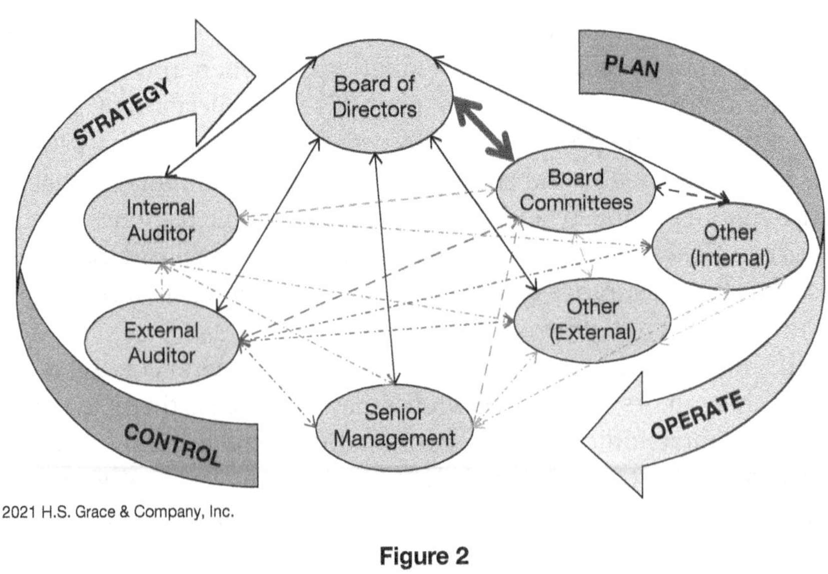

Figure 2

First, we examine the forces that are driving this evolution of board and board committee responsibilities; second, we examine the current state of board and board committee responsibilities; and third, we address board-management relationships and offer certain conclusions. We start by considering the forces driving the evolution because, to understand these responsibilities—where board and board committees are today and where they will be tomorrow—we must look at the framework within which their current roles and responsibilities have evolved.

The increased focus on boards and board committee responsibilities did not occur in a vacuum. This increased focus is the result of deep-seated forces at work in the areas of personal, political, and organization governance. These subtle, yet powerful, forces are the underlying currents driving the tides of change in the world in which we live.

When we examine the forces at work in the areas of personal, political, and organization governance, what we see is remarkable—actually fascinating! The forces there have been building for hundreds, if not thousands, of years and represent a continuing evolution.

With an understanding of the evolving personal and political framework, we then examine the current state of board and board committee responsibilities within organizations and explore the implications for boards, board committees, and senior management going forward. The conclusions forthcoming are interesting and straightforward.

Importantly, change is ongoing because there is a framework for change in place that is explicit and unequivocal in both its demand for an increased level of responsibility from board committees, boards, and senior management, and in its requirement that board and management positions be understood to be positions of service and not entitlement or privilege. The change that is ongoing is that board and board committee responsibilities will broaden and deepen; and boards, board committees, and senior management will be subject to increased scrutiny, as we have discussed above with respect to the *Caremark* line of decisions. The framework for change sets out:

- an explicit and unequivocal demand for an increased level of responsibility from board committees, boards, and senior management, and
- an explicit requirement that board and management positions be understood to be positions of service and not of entitlement.

Let us be clear, this framework of change driving the evolution of board responsibilities is not ours. It arises from the writings and thinking of social scientists, political scientists, spiritualists, philosophers, and lo and behold, economists. The views of these thinkers point toward both individual investors and the institutions representing these investors becoming more demanding of boards, management, and board committees in their roles as participants in the organization governance process.

Both the company's law department and its outside counsel have a critical role in this process. Keeping in mind that in-house counsel's sole client is the company itself, it is incumbent on that counsel to advise the company to have the optimal corporate governance structure in place and implemented on a going forward basis. Outside counsel may have a bit different role, particularly where they are retained specifically to advise the board and/or executive management.

Many of these situations lead to derivative litigation where the defendants may be (1) individual board members, (2) individual officers, at the C-Suite level, and (3) the corporation, which is typically only a nominal defendant. Although nominal only, the corporation has a real interest in the litigation. In certain situations, it may even have the right to take over prosecution of the litigation.

There can also be real conflicts between the officer defendants and independent board member defendants. All of this suggests counsel to represent these differing interests is critical.

In examining the forces at work, in personal governance, political governance, and organization governance, we note these forces operate both in sequence and in parallel. The fundamental building block is personal governance. It is the building block that has driven the evolution of political and organizational governance. Thus, we begin by looking at the forces at work in the area of personal governance, the fundamental long-standing forces that drive the individuals who comprise organizations.

1. Personal Governance

The forces moving through the area of personal governance are fundamentally the forces driving individual lives—the forces driving how individuals govern themselves. Personal governance issues have existed for millennia and the following is illustrative of the foundations of this governance.

Long ago, Socrates asked, "What is the good life?", and this question of what a good life is, has received considerable attention over the centuries. Let us look at some of the answers. Aristotle set out that man's greatest joy comes from giving of himself and his possessions to others:

> *" . . . there is the greatest pleasure in doing a kindness or service to friends or guests or companions, which can only be rendered when a man has private property." . . .Politics, Book Two, Chapter Five.*

Three hundred years before Aristotle, Isaiah called on us to share our possessions and ourselves.

> *"Thus says the Lord: Share your bread with the hungry, shelter the oppressed and the homeless; clothe the naked when you see them, and do not turn your back on your own. If you bestow your bread on the hungry and satisfy the*

afflicted; Then light shall rise for you in the darkness, and the gloom shall become for you like midday"...... Isaiah 58: 7–10 (74)

At the time of Isaiah, or perhaps as much as 600 years earlier, from the east came the Tao, which sets out that the more the master does for others, the happier he is, and that the more the master gives to others, the wealthier he is.

"The Master has no possessions. The more he does for others, the happier he is. The more he gives to others, the wealthier he is."

Moving forward in time, the powerful words of Immanuel Kant call for the recognition of a moral law within each of us—a set of values:

"Two things fill the mind with ever new and interesting admiration and awe: the starry heavens above and the moral law within. . . I see them before me and connect them directly with the consciousness of my existence."

Then, there is Carl Jung discussing what happens when individuals fail to follow this moral law.

"Among all patients in the second half of life—that is, to say over 35—It is safe to say that every one of them fell ill because he had lost that which the living religions of every age have given to their followers, and none of them has been really healed who did not regain his religious outlook. This of course has nothing whatever to do with a particular creed or membership of a church."....... "Psychotherapists or the Clergy," Modern Man in Search of a Soul

And as we move to current times, there is Mother Teresa's Simple Path, which is said to have been printed by a Muslim gentleman first.

The Simple Path
The fruit of Silence is Prayer.
The fruit of Prayer is Faith.
The fruit of Faith is Love.
The fruit of Love is Service.
The fruit of Service is Peace.

Look closely at the last two steps: "The fruit of love is service, and the fruit of service is peace."

Over thousands of years, these individuals have pointed us to maximizing our economic wellbeing and not our financial wellbeing. We could ask, "Do individuals follow that guidance?"

Nobel economist Robert W. Fogel addresses this in his outstanding work, *The Fourth Great Awakening: The Future of Egalitarianism in America.* Fogel has produced powerful insights into the personal lives of our country's citizens. Fogel carefully pointed out the long-term twentieth century trend of individuals spending less time earning wages which, in turn, can be used to purchase material possessions. Instead, individuals are seeking increased time to acquire what Fogel called the non-material or spiritual goods—time with their families, in their communities, or at their synagogues, mosques, and churches:

- *Profound long-term trends*
- *Reduced earnwork: wages, material possessions*
- *Increased volwork: personal time, nonmaterial, and spiritual goods*

Fogel is quick to point out that he is not moralizing. In fact, outside his book, he has mentioned that he had not been a member of a formal religion since age 13, at which time his father told him his religion was in his own hands. Fogel simply points out the unmistakable trend of individuals spending more time in volwork, and less time in earnwork. His analysis of the data establishes that, in large measure, individuals in this country have found that the quality of their lives is increased more by these volwork activities than by the earnwork activities which would increase their financial income and their possession of material goods.

What Fogel is saying is critically important—that is, that individuals seek to maximize utility (personal satisfaction), and this is distinctly different than maximizing financial wealth. This is what economists have always taught; that economic well-being is not equal to financial well-being. Fogel points out that individuals recognize, by their behavior, exactly what economists have said, and what philosophers and spiritualists have said, and did so even before economics as a science existed.

What Fogel, other economists, and philosophers are saying is that, while most of us may be financially better off than either Mother Teresa or her sisters, they may be much better off economically than we are. That is, the degree of personal satisfaction, the utility that they derive from the lives that they have chosen to live may, and more than likely does, far exceed the level of utility or satisfaction we have derived from our own lives.

What is important is that board members and management including counsel recognize the manner in which their firm's employees and related personnel are making decisions.

In his book, Fogel gives us a useful example of this measurement of personal satisfaction with two toolmakers, John and Harry (Figure 3). John and Harry each earn twenty dollars per hour. John works only 1,800 hours per work year, taking advantage of short workweeks, long weekends, and many vacations. Accordingly, John's annual income is $36,000 and his projected retirement age is sixty-five.

A TALE OF TWO TOOLMAKERS

	JOHN	HARRY
Annual Income	$36,000	$64,000
Age	45	45
Hourly Wage	$20.00	$20.00
Workyear (Hours)	1,800	3,200
Planned Retirement Age	65	55
Work Preferences	• Short workweek • Long weekends • Month-long vacation	• Long workweek • Overtime • Minimal vacation
Volwork	• Time with family • Active in his religion • Coaches son's little league team	• Very little volwork currently • Plans more volwork after retirement

Figure 3

However, his choices permit John to pursue several volwork activities with his family, at his church, and in his community. For Harry, is an earlier retirement age: fifty-five, a higher income: $64,000, and many more earnwork pursuits. Harry works longer hours, weeks, etc. and has less time presently for volwork. Both men have similar cumulative life-cycle earnings and hours. But they have chosen much different lifestyles. John's leisure hour distribution will reach into in his early to mid-adulthood years, while Harry's leisure hours will be concentrated in later life. John and Harry have selected different approaches to financial well-being to maximize their *economic well-being.*

An actual example of Fogel's findings occurred in New York City in the 1990s. Senior financial executives as members of the Public Interest Initiatives Committee (PIIC) of the New York City (NYC) Chapter of the Financial Executives International (FEI) made the decision to use their experience and skills to help make New York City a better place to live and work.[2] The FEI chapter put in place a set of guidelines that precluded assistance in both fundraising and goal setting and focused on non-monetary assistance in achieving the goals set by the city, state and other organizations. Again, the FEI members were not involved in setting the goals of these organizations, nor in fund raising.

[2] Financial Executives International (FEI) is an organization of senior financial executives of companies over a certain size or otherwise qualifying, non-profit and government organizations, and certain academics active in finance. FEI is recognized as the spoke person for business and industry on issues of finance, accounting, and financial management. Its membership is at approximately 10,000 members.

If one asks what the most precious resources of these FEI members are, the answer would be their time and their energy. It is certainly easier for most of them to write someone a check than it is to give of their time and energy. But let's look at what the PIIC Committee elected to do. Its work included several projects with the Office of the New York State Comptroller, projects with the City University of New York (CUNY), the City of New York, Hunter College, the U.S. Government CFO's Council, the United Nations, the Archdiocese of New York Schools, Baruch College, the New York State Fire Chiefs Association and unions representing the firemen and women. A broad range of projects was undertaken on which PIIC members shared their knowledge and experience.

The NYC FEI chapter surveyed its members to determine what drove these executives to participate? When one looks at what members of the chapter had to say about their work, the powerful impact of their experiences make clear that this was a win-win for all parties.

These comments of the FEI members support Fogel's findings, and are quite close, if not identical, to the life targets we saw advocated earlier by philosophers and spiritualists:

- "I have participated in chapter board meetings for years at which we discuss membership and programs. Now we are addressing important topics."
- "We cannot just have monthly meetings at which we eat and talk. We must do something worthwhile."
- "I have been a member for over ten years. This is the most important thing the chapter has ever done."
- "We must do this work."

Both the business community and society in general responded to the New York FEI chapter's work. One of the authors delivered "The Role of the CFO in Public Policy—Wanted: A Few Good CFOs" to Forbes Special CFO Forum in 1997. "The Corporate Report" published a detailed review of the address, which is reprinted here in appendix I as it is out of print.

"Gaining From Giving: The Benefits of Corporate Volunteerism" was delivered to CFO magazine's "CFO Rising 1999" conference. This followed CFO magazine's August 1997 cover story "A Higher Reward—Volunteerism Attracts a New Breed of 'Financial Angel.'"

What we have is philosophers, spiritualists, psychologists, and economists, all speaking the same language, and these senior financial executives living the language. Just as economists have set out that what individuals seek is to maximize their personal utility or the personal satisfaction they gain from life, philosophers, spiritualists, and psychologists have been advocating what actions individuals should take, what goals individuals should pursue in their personal lives, if in fact they are going to maximize their personal utility. An interesting case concerning senior executives of one of the largest U.S. firms is discussed in chapter VII. It should not surprise us that Adam Smith, the father of economics, was a professor of moral philosophy.

Returning to Fogel's work because what he is saying is so important to boards and senior management, Fogel points out that in the third great awakening the equal distribution of material possessions was incorrectly thought to lead to equality among individuals. However, just as the examples here demonstrate, material possessions do not determine economic equality. Fogel's work clarifies those non-material, spiritual resources that he feels must be properly distributed among people if the goal of equality is to be achieved: sense of purpose (maybe the most important); vision of opportunity; a sense of the mainstream of work and life; a strong family ethic; a sense of community; a capacity to engage with diverse groups; an ethic of benevolence; a work ethic; a sense of discipline; the capacity to focus and concentrate one's efforts; a capacity to resist the lure of hedonism; a capacity for self-education; a thirst for knowledge; an appreciation for quality; and, finally, self-esteem (which Fogel believes is required for the assimilation for all of the others).

What Fogel is saying is that his research indicates that, if we are going to achieve economic equality, individuals must have access to these resources. He goes on to discuss how to address the issues of access. Fogel's work has implications for many social policy issues that are addressed each day on the personal, the political, and the business level. As an organization's people reach out to assist, to share, this is important to keep in mind.

We can see a direct connection between the forces at work in personal governance and the responsibilities of management, boards, and board committees. Very simply, the more effective management, boards and board committees are in addressing their responsibilities, the greater the financial and non-financial return to shareholders. The financial success aids employees and shareholders to improve the quality of their lives as they choose between volwork and earnwork. A firm able to create opportunities carefully and appropriately for volwork can experience the employee success achieved by the NYC FEI member firms. This is not revolutionary, but it is irrefutable. It is a fundamental fact that provides the basis for individual investors and the institutions representing them to make clear to management, boards, and board committees that they have accepted positions of responsibility and of service and are expected to ensure those shareholders and others fully receive the fruits of their labors/investments.

We turn now to the forces at work in political governance.

2. Political Governance

We (the authors) have always been attracted to this area of activity—society's choice of political governance systems. Our interest includes an exchange between one of the authors many years ago, with Paul Samuelson in the "The Quarterly Journal of Economics" (QJE) (set out here in Appendix II). The exchange examined issues regarding the proper form of political and economic governance for a unique volcanic island economy. The primary point was, while Samuelson and the author initially differed, ultimately they agreed on certain, inherent difficulties facing a centrally planned governance structure in contrast to a competitively based governance structure. As an aside, Professor Samuelson's contributions to the field have been immense. It was a compliment for the author to receive a letter from QJE informing him Samuelson agreed with and expanded his findings and that his note and Samuelson's reply would be published.[3] The political governance issues addressed in the exchange are directly applicable to issues facing the Chinese government and other centrally planned economies attempting to go forward, issues we believe to deserve the careful consideration of boards, management, and corporate governance counsel.

The history of political governance, for the most part, has been the history of kings, monarchs, and dictators. But throughout this history, structural stresses and troublesome issues appeared continually. Aristotle's quote about the primary source of mankind's joy arose in the context of his opposition to the call of both Socrates and Plato for broad-based state ownership of property. Marcus Aurelius in his "Meditations" discusses challenging aspects of political governance, and Thomas More in *Utopia*, cleverly set out a form of government sharply different from what existed in the world at the time.

The basic problem that continued to arise was the consistent failure in the tone at the top of monarchies and dictatorships. Going back to the Biblical days, there was an oft-heard call for a king who would save the people from whatever problems confronted them (for example, the Book of Samuel). Yet those wishing for such an arrangement kept finding out that this form of political governance was not working, and it wasn't working in very fundamental ways: basic equality, as well as recognition of and respect for the rights of individuals, was missing. Individuals opposing those in power would disappear, women could and would be taken and abused. There was a consistent pattern of fundamental human rights abuse, however these might have been discerned at some point. So, conceptually, while a monarchy or dictatorship possessed the potential to be an efficient, effective form of political governance, there was a proven record of failure.

Certainly, there have been monarchs and dictators widely recognized for their achievements over the centuries. Interestingly, these individuals appear to have exhibited a common set of values seemingly centered around recognition of their role as servants to the country they led; and their governance was based on fundamentals that recognized and respected individual rights.

Throughout history, mankind has searched for a form of government that respects and protects the rights of individuals, a form that treasures these inherent rights and values. And then, in 1776 fifty-five men put their names on a document

[3] A summary of which is set out in Appendix II.

that proclaimed, "We believe these truths to be self-evident. . ." The experiment we know as democracy was underway—again, not occurring in a vacuum, but as an event in the continuum of man's search for an appropriate structure of political governance. However, just as the Rev. Richard John Neuhaus said so eloquently in his book, *Doing Well and Doing Good*, democracy is a continuing experiment, and, as he said further, the ideas of freedom need to be thought through and given fresh expression with each generation. Why? Because the day our form of government ceases to recognize, respect, and protect the rights of the individuals, the day it fails to recognize and respect the moral laws—the inherent values and rights within its citizens, it will fall from favor within the hearts of its citizens, and a search for a new form of government will be underway.

The forces at work in political governance send strong messages to boards, board committees, and senior management. The demand that individual rights be recognized and respected underpins the call for an increased level of responsibility for the board, board committees, and management. Further, the fact that the convergence of power and authority into too few hands, while seeming efficient, consistently failed, points to the need for board and board committees' role in the governance, the oversight, and the management of the organization.

To summarize, the confluence of forces in the areas of personal and political governance has strong implications for the governance of organizations.

3. Organization Governance

Let us open our examination of organization governance repeating the thoughtful words of Courtney Brown, dean of a leading business school some fifty years ago, who was also an author and a director of multiple major corporations:

> *"Members of governing boards have a prestigious status in society—more prestigious than the present nature of their activities can support. It is a status that reflects the popular belief and expectation that governing boards do indeed govern. . . Building on that popular belief and expectation, the work of governing boards can and should be clarified and strengthened to the ultimate benefit of corporations of all kinds and of society at large."*

This quote is from the preface of his book, *Putting Corporate Boards to Work*, published in 1976, his words evidence the ongoing, long-standing, awareness of board governance deficiencies.

Look at the concluding words in Brown's quote ". . . the work of governing boards can and should be clarified and strengthened to the ultimate benefit of corporations of all kinds and of society at large." These are words about the benefits of service—the service of boards to the corporation, non-corporate organizations and to society—shareholders, employees, customers, and so forth.

Just as democracy is a continuing experiment, the evolution of organization governance within a democracy is a subset of that experiment. One should not forget that the public and private sectors are linked tightly. The private sector flourishes if the public sector works. If the public sector is weak, the private sector will struggle.

And just as the ideas of freedom need to be thought through and given fresh expression, the ideas of organization governance must be reexamined continually as well.

Experience has shown, governance structures that consolidate power and authority into fewer and fewer hands, while conceptually attractive in terms of their efficiency and effectiveness, have consistently failed to meet their conceptual ideals. Yet, in the face of this experience and wisdom, it appears in the areas of both corporate and non-corporate governance, we continue to hear the call for improving the tone at the top—for raising the quality of senior management. Saying the solution to improved organization governance is improving only the quality of senior management ignores history's lessons. An improved organization governance process is necessary—an improved set of checks and balances that defines responsibilities, demands accountability, and carries consequences. These checks and balances involve the dynamic defining of the roles and responsibilities of all of the participants in the governance process—not just senior management.

Lord Acton said, "Power corrupts, and absolute power corrupts absolutely." The Roman poet Ovid framed the situation well, some two thousand years ago, when he said, "The better things of life I see and approve, the worse things of life I follow." Their words insightfully reflect the breakdowns we see in those governance structures where power has been consolidated into a few hands. Their words provide the backdrop for understanding the failures in the tone at the top.

This leads us to an important point. Organization governance is not a zero-sum game. The work of Von Neumann and Morgenstern and the other game theorists notwithstanding, the structure and operation of a governance process is not a zero-sum exercise. Organization governance is not about shifting power from one participant to another. This is about the dynamic definition of the roles and responsibilities of each and every participant in a manner that optimizes potential synergies. Organization governance is a win-win or a lose-lose situation—not just for the participants, but all of society.

Let's draw from Rev. Neuhaus again about another issue concerning organization governance—we must be careful not to consider human greed and foolishness, which have been evident always and everywhere, an indictment of a capitalist system. A properly functioning organization governance process in the democratic capitalism we know puts in place a set of checks and balances that helps to mitigate these forces of human greed and foolishness and encourages responsible action on the part of all involved parties. This properly functioning organization governance process encourages senior management, board members, and all involved parties to approach their positions with a sense of responsibility and an attitude of service.

At this point, we can begin to sense the confluence of the various underlying forces that recognize the rights of individual investors to the fruits of their labor. Institutions who represent investors are increasingly showing a keen awareness of this. Certainly, there may be dialogue and disagreement as to how best to realize and protect these rights, but there can be no disagreement as to the existence and importance of these rights.

To put it simply, the coalescing of individual investors and their institutional representatives which is occurring focuses the paths of corporate and non-corporate governance along the road from entitlement to service.

It is critical for a lawyer to understand the interests of all these constituencies, including the investors who in most cases will be adverse to the lawyer's own clients. A lawyer can deliver optimal counsel only when he or she appreciates the interests of all constituencies.

4. Board and Board Committees

Looking at boards and their responsibilities, obtaining an understanding of the long-term forces at work in the areas of personal, political, and organization governance is very helpful. Further, the focus on boards and board committees and the attention being paid to clarifying their roles and responsibilities within the organization governance process is no surprise.

The increased focus on board and board committees is real, and it is appropriate. The buck stops with senior management, the board, and board committees, and their roles and interrelationships must be defined and understood. Next to a firm examining where they are and determining where they want to go, one of the most challenging tasks confronting a firm is ensuring that an effective oversight and control system is in place. The board, with and through its board committees, has the utmost responsibility for ensuring the quality and integrity of the system.

Figure 2, introduced earlier in this chapter, distinguishes those challenges, which differ in each organization and can differ over time. It is within Figure 2 that the interrelationships are determined and the checks and balances and required transparency are put in place.

Recognizing the existence of these responsibilities carries with it the challenge of addressing them. Such a situation, which one of the authors experienced, underscores these challenges. In his role as CFO of a large holding company, he was responsible for more than sixty subsidiaries, joint ventures, and affiliated companies. The portfolio included ownership of an NBA team, a team in the World Hockey League, an indoor soccer team, involvement in the cable TV business, computerized ticketing, a large leasing company, and many other operations. One of those operations was a real estate development subsidiary, for which he was also CFO. At that time, the real estate subsidiary was one of the largest development companies in the world. The organizational forms included parent-subsidiary corporations, limited and general partnerships, LLCs, and joint ventures. Despite continual interaction with these operations, the challenges of understanding their complexities were substantial.

Equally or more complicated is the role of a board member in such a firm, tasked with trying to understand and monitor these diverse operations. To say the least—it is a daunting task, and yet one that many boards and their committees face today.

Despite the challenges, these board-related responsibilities can be addressed. A successful and effective board and board committees can not only do the right thing, but also create a roadmap to address times of complexity.

A key resource is the firm's legal counsel, internal and external, and if necessary, counsel to the board. A key step is stress testing the organizational structure.

II. Stress Testing Your Organization Governance Structure

The governance bells are tolling for corporate, non-corporate, not-for-profit, governmental, and other organizations. Investor and stakeholder demands, regulatory actions, and growing litigation risks are contributing to the focus on management and director responsibilities for effective governance. The personal and political governance evolution supports this increased focus. Therefore, there is the need to stress test governance structures and examine the viability of the existing checks and balances, to review the increased focus on board governance and oversight responsibilities, and to explore opportunities to create governance structures with a harder edge, while continuing to recognize governance's often pivotal role in litigation. While exemplary organization governance practices cannot eliminate all instances of legal action, a sound governance structure will enhance the ability to successfully defend against such suits, aiming for an early resolution through motions to dismiss or summary judgment.

The importance of effective organization governance and key considerations in assessing governance merit ongoing, if not continual, attention. Resources for gaining a deeper understanding of these issues should be explored as well.

A. Stress Testing Governance Structures: An Introduction

1. Strategy-Plan-Operate-Control Cycle

Figure 2, discussed previously, sets out the basic governance structure of an organization.

Stress testing determines the effectiveness of the governance structure in addressing the needs of the particular organization at that point in time. Stress testing examines how, and how well, an organization's management and board are directing current operations and their level of preparedness to react to specific risks and challenges. Those challenges may stem from various sources, such as business competition, economic events and conditions, regulatory inquiries, changing shareowner expectations, litigation, or other causes. Stress testing examines the responsibilities of corporate governance lawyers and analyzes how those responsibilities are being addressed.

This is not a middle market situation. The need for effective stress testing is exemplified in high profile cases such as the breakdowns in the governance structures of Wells Fargo, Blue Bell (Marchand), and Boeing, among others. This focus on the governance structure goes back to, and beyond, the well-known Walt Disney Shareholder Derivative Litigation (Disney) involving the hiring (and subsequent termination) of Michael Ovitz. That case addressed a plaintiff estimated $130 million termination package delivered to Ovitz, after fourteen months of disappointing performance at the company.

At that time, Disney was referred to as the corporate governance case of the century. The court made the board's responsibilities for governance and oversight clear, and examined how Disney management and its board addressed those responsibilities, as Chancellor Chandler said, reviewing each individual director's performance. The Disney litigation was eye-opening to many in the corporate sector because previously, it was presumed that the business judgment rule defense would bring a quick end to the litigation. The Delaware Supreme Court did not see it that way and remanded the case to the lower court where the derivative suit would be tried on the merits. Ultimately, the Disney directors prevailed, but only after incurring significant legal defense expense. *In re The Walt Disney Co. Derivative Litigation*, 907 A 2d 693 (Del. 2005) was a landmark decision, that upheld the business judgment rule affording directors wide latitude in their decision making.

We have authored four articles on our work in *Disney*, the first article was "An Insider Revisits the 'Disney Case'" (*Directors Monthly*, August 2008).[4] All of the articles discuss issues that came up in the litigation, draws on the work of outstanding jurists, and addresses issues with ongoing implications for organization governance. In certain respects, the articles constitute a snapshot of "The Rest of the Disney Litigation Story."

Also noteworthy was derivative litigation involving Wells Fargo & Company. *In re Wells Fargo & Company Shareholder Derivative Litigation*, United States District Court for the Northern District of California, Case No. 16-cv-05541. On April 7, 2020, Judge Jon S. Tigar of the Northern District of California granted final approval to a settlement including a $240 million cash payment and corporate governance reforms. At the time, the settlement was the largest insurer-funded derivative settlement in history.

[4] The other articles "Plaintiff Expert Reports—An Insider Revisits Disney," *NYSBA Journal*, July/August 2009; "Governance Lessons from the Disney Litigation," *Business Law Today*, September 2011; "Corporate Governance—Lessons From Life and Litigation—With Implications for Corporate Counsel," *NYSBA Journal*, March/April 2013.

The Wells Fargo litigation involves serious allegations against the board and executive management of Wells Fargo. The plaintiffs allege that, since at least 2011, the Wells Fargo board and executive management knew or consciously disregarded that Wells Fargo employees were illicitly creating millions of deposit and credit card accounts for their customers, without the consent of those customers, in an attempt to drive up cross-selling, i.e., selling complementary Wells Fargo banking products to prospective or existing customers.

Associated litigation has been ongoing with costs estimated in the billions.

2. From Tone at the Top to Checks and Balances

The concept of tone at the top as the guiding hand of an organization's governance structure—where tone at the top took the form of a CEO/Chair governing and managing the organization and the board being relegated to oversight—is still valued but emphasized less now. Today, there is broad-based recognition of the need for the appropriate checks and balances positioned in an environment characterized by transparency. The 2002 *CPA Journal* article "From Tone at the Top to Checks and Balances"[5] authored by members of the Grace & Co. Board of Advisors, and the 2004 *Wall Street Journal* op-ed[6] where Paul Volcker and Arthur Levitt Jr. point to the breakdown in checks and balances as the fundamental cause of major corporate collapses such as Enron and WorldCom both contributed to this evolving view of governance, which is further discussed here in chapter III "From Tone at the Top to Checks and Balances."

B. Board Governance: The Fed and Wells Fargo; Blue Bell and Boeing

The 2018 Order to Cease and Desist between the Board of Governors of the Federal Reserve and the Board of Wells Fargo, along with recent developments concerning Boeing and Blue Bell Ice Cream, demonstrates the current state of board, board committee, and senior management business duties to govern, oversee, and manage. Senator Elizabeth Warren's letter to Federal Reserve Chairman Jerome H. Powell urging a revocation of the bank's operating license and forcing a break-up splitting the banking operations from Wells Fargo's other financial and investment services was further evidence of the nature of the problems.

Our 2019 article "Board Oversight and Governance: From Tone at the Top to Substantive Checks and Balances," along with the writings of former Delaware Supreme Court Chief Justice Norman Veasey and former Delaware Court of Chancery Chancellor William Chandler contributes significantly to the perspective that the board of directors will actually direct and monitor the management

[5] "From 'Tone at the Top' To 'Checks and Balances,'" by James N. Clark, R. Hartwell Gardner, H. Stephen Grace, Jr., John E. Haupert and Robert S. Roath, *The CPA Journal*, March 2002.

[6] Paul Volcker and Arthur Levitt, Jr., "In Defense of Sarbanes-Oxley" *Wall Street Journal*, June 14, 2004.

of the company. Delaware law is clear—the business and affairs of a corporation are managed by or under the direction of its board of directors. A leading decision discussing the propriety of setting an appropriate tone at the top in guiding company employees is *Hertz Corp. v. Frissora* Civil Action No. 19-8927 (ES) (CLW) UNITED STATES DISTRICT COURT DISTRICT OF NEW JERSEY Decided June 3, 2021.

In his May 2005 *University of Pennsylvania Law Review* article, Chief Justice Veasey stated, "The board of directors will actually direct and monitor the management of the company, including strategic business and fundamental structural changes." Chancellor Chandler, in his opinion in the Disney Shareholder Derivative Litigation, stated, "Delaware law is clear that the business and affairs of a corporation are managed by or under the direction of its Board of Directors."

The Federal Reserve website describes a board's responsibility to create and enforce prudent policies and practices with the following statement: "Directors are placed in a position of trust by the bank's shareholders, and both statutes and common law place responsibility for the affairs of a bank firmly and squarely on the board of directors. The board of directors of a bank should delegate the day-to-day routine of conducting the bank's business to its officers and employees, but the board cannot delegate its responsibility for the consequences of unsound or imprudent policies and practices."

The recent Delaware shareholder derivative action involving Boeing is illustrative of a board's oversight responsibilities. See *In re The Boeing Company Derivative Litigation*, 2021 WL 4059934 (Del. Ch. Sept. 7, 2021). This decision from the Delaware Chancery Court arose from the Boeing board's conduct before and after two crashes of its 737 Max aircraft. The decision serves as a cautionary tale for directors regarding the importance of board and board committee level governance, oversight, and monitoring of mission critical product safety risks.

C. Governance's Often Pivotal Role in Litigation

Governance issues, which encompass plaintiffs and defendants, can occupy a pivotal role in litigation. The December 2016 *Business Law Today (BLT)* article "The Interplay between Corporate Governance issues and Litigation: What is Corporate Governance and How Does It Affect Litigation" and the September 2011 *BLT* article "Governance Lessons from the Disney Litigation" demonstrate the importance of stress testing an entity's governance structure as part of minimizing litigation.[7] Actual cases, and the value of examining these cases under a business lens, are explored in these articles and are commended to the reader.

[7] H. Stephen Grace, John E. Haupert and Susan Koski-Grafer, *Business Law Today*, December 2016. and H. Stephen Grace and John E. Haupert, "Governance Lessons from the Disney Litigation", *Business Law Today*, September 2011.

D. Putting the Governance Structure Under the Microscope

1. Revisiting the Division of Labor

A fundamental economic guidepost outlined in *Management 101* and *Introduction to Organization Behavior* is that the division of labor is specific to an organization at a point in time. Two organizations, even if controlled by the same parties and appearing identical in many respects, may be organized and operated quite differently.

The belief that organizational and operational issues can be addressed simply by adopting best practices overlooks and neglects the unique governance, oversight, and management issues that an organization can face at any point in time. Boards, board committees, management, and the corporate governance lawyer must work together to address the fundamental responsibilities set out in Figure 1. They should put their collectively developed approaches to work within the Strategy-Plan-Operate-Control Cycle of the organization shown in Figure 2.

2. Stress-testing the Corporate Governance Structure

Stress testing an organization's governance structure is not without sensitivities. Engage a deeply experienced, properly positioned third party who understands these sensitivities to assist. A fundamental early step involves an organization understanding its current position and future objectives. While it may seem straightforward, there can be a range of perspectives about where an organization is, and where an organization aspires to go.

In an organization, there can be differences of opinion about the organization's current position as well as the desired future position of the organization.

The board and board committee roles in addressing such fundamental issues are not only important, but continue to grow in importance. A case summary that involves the good, the bad, and the ugly that can arise in governance structures follows.

3. The Good, the Bad, and the Ugly

Organization governance is dynamic and complex. The dynamics require ongoing attention, and the complexities are challenging. The following real-world case with names changed to protect confidentiality of the involved parties captures the good, the bad, and the ugly elements that can and do arise.

In this case, X Bank, a large bank, acquired ABC Savings. In doing so X Bank acquired a lawsuit filed against ABC Savings by the Y State Public Employees' Retirement System (YPERS) in connection with their loss of $75 million dollars, which had been invested in a capital note and two subordinated debentures. YPERS had invested in a capital note and two subordinated debentures issued by ABC Savings, a federally charted capital stock savings and loan association, in a total principal amount of $75 million dollars. Defendant, X Bank, served as the indenture trustee, under two trust indentures for the two debentures (the two trust indentures are collectively referred to as the Indentures). Subsequently, the Resolution Trust Corporation placed ABC Savings in receivership, resulting in a total loss of YPERS' investment.

X Bank, the client of H.S. Grace & Co. as its expert consultant in this matter, served as indenture trustee in connection with two subordinated debentures of $40 million and $20 million. A $15 million investment in the capital note did not involve X Bank directly, but YPERS's position was that, if X Bank had fulfilled its responsibilities, the $15 million would also have been recovered. Despite some adverse rulings from the court on issues presented on motions for summary judgment, X Bank ultimately prevailed as explained below.

X Bank's position was complicated by the following three factors:

1. X Bank laid off several people in the town where the trial was to be held (in State District Court) after the acquisition of the local bank.
2. X Bank realized that the lawyers for YPERS may implicitly or explicitly convey to the jury that, if X Bank is not found liable for the losses, the alternative will be for the taxes of the state's citizens to be increased to replace the lost funds; and
3. X Bank had a witness problem. The senior individuals who managed the Trust Department of the local bank were deceased, and the only individual left from the Trust Department was a young man no longer in the banking business. He was in the lawn maintenance business, with a somewhat unruly appearance, and did not fare well in his deposition in explaining the actions taken by the local bank in connection with its role as trustee.

YPERS's Board of Trustees was comprised of non-professional citizen volunteers who lacked significant investment experience. The board was therefore expected to retain professionals to advise it and to prudently manage YPERS's investments. Because of its putative skill and experience in the administration of trusts, X Bank was retained to serve as the Indenture Trustee for both the $40 million and $20 million ABC Savings debentures. As the Indenture Trustee, X Bank was to act for the benefit of YPERS. With the retention of X Bank, YPERS received a vehicle to protect $60 million dollars of its investment in ABC Savings. When it assumed its role as indenture trustee, X Bank knowingly undertook contractual and fiduciary obligations to YPERS. YPERS alleged that X Bank dismally failed in these obligations. YPERS's alleged the following:

Under the trust indenture, X Bank was obligated to examine certain reports ABC Savings provided. If a report suggested the existence of a default event, X Bank had to notify YPERS of a potential default and investigate properly. If X Bank determined there had been an event of default, it was obligated to take appropriate steps to protect YPERS's interest, including declaring the accrued interest and principal of the subordinated indentures to be due and payable immediately. For a critical period, ABC Savings issued annual reports to X Bank that disclosed that ABC Savings entered a series of transactions in direct violation of its covenants in the two trust indentures. X Bank did not investigate the suspect transactions, did not notify YPERS of any actual or potential event of default, and did not accelerate payment of principal and accrued interest of the subordinated debentures. YPERS alleged X Bank's failure to perform its duties under the trust indenture resulted in YPERS' loss of its entire investment in ABC Savings, including the $60 million dollars it had invested under the two trust indentures.

In a nutshell, X Bank argued that it is entitled to judgment because it undertook only a "limited ministerial role" to "collect reports and payments from the issuer of the debentures," ABC Savings, and that it discharged its duties fully by relying "on annual certificates from ABC Savings confirming its compliance with all provisions in the Indenture Agreements." YPERS countered, however, that these annual certificates, known as officers' certificates, were untimely, facially insufficient, and non-compliant with the indentures. YPERS stated X Bank's reliance on officers' certificates were, as a matter of law, a drastic breach of their contractual and common law fiduciary duties as indenture trustee.

X Bank argued that its failure to fulfill its duties as an indenture trustee and apprise YPERS of ABC Savings' numerous, unlawful transactions with affiliated banks was not the cause of YPERS' loss. This was based on the contention that the knowledge YPERS' investment manager possessed regarding those affiliated transactions and other questionable ABC Savings activities is imputed to YPERS. However, YPERS countered by asserting that Y state law will not impute the knowledge of an adverse agent to its principal, and the investment manager was as adverse as an agent could get. X Bank's argument that YPERS was estopped from suing it for its lack of performance because YPERS never instructed it to fulfill its duty and declare an Event of Default also was challenged. As shown below, estoppel cannot be imposed on a state instrumentality acting in its governmental capacity. Furthermore, X Bank cannot establish a single element of estoppel, particularly because, according to the very terms of the Indentures, YPERS waived none of its claims against X Bank. Additionally, YPERS did not relinquish any of its claims against X Bank when it tried to mitigate its damages by exchanging its worthless ABC Savings debentures for worthless ABC Savings debentures for equally worthless ABC Savings stock.

On the contrary, the court noted there is no genuine issue of material fact indicating X Bank assumed an obligation to examine ABC Savings' officers' certificates to determine their compliance with the terms of the indenture. There is no genuine issue of material fact that the officers' certificates failed to adhere to the terms of the indenture. Simply stated, if X Bank had fulfilled its contractual duty to examine the officers' certificates for conformity with the requirements of the indenture, it would have discovered ABC Savings' numerous defaults, allowing YPERS to take prompt measures to avoid its losses.

X Bank had direct knowledge of ABC Savings' defaults, distinct from its fraudulent officers' certificates. Documents X Bank collected and maintained as indenture trustee established that ABC Savings repeatedly violated the terms of the Indentures in several respects. Notably, X Bank received ABC Savings' annual reports and an offering circular describing its proposed merger with DEF Savings & Loan These documents revealed ABC Savings' participation in tens of millions of dollars of prohibited affiliated transactions, violations that ABC Savings itself acknowledged (in the very documents tendered to X Bank) as contravening federal banking regulations. By law, X Bank was required to act as a prudent person to protect YPERS's interest. There is no genuine issue of material fact that X Bank failed to act, much less acted imprudently. X Bank's failure to fulfill its obligations under the indentures constituted a breach of its contractual and fiduciary duties to YPERS. If X Bank had acted in accordance with its obligations, YPERS could have voided its transactions with ABC Savings and recouped its entire principal investment.

In the final resolution of the dispute between YPERS and X Bank, X Bank leveraging the analysis its expert consultant provided, successfully convinced YPERS to dismiss its claims against the bank. YPERS continued to litigate against other defendants and recovered a total of $100 million from those other defendants who were not aware of X Bank's expert consultant's findings. X Bank did not make any payments to YPERS in the course of this resolution.

The management expert found serious shortcomings on the part of both YPERS and X Bank. However, X Bank's oversight did not cause YPERS's losses. Governance breakdowns within YPERS were critical and ultimately, led to the voluntary dismissal of its suit against X Bank.

III. Evolving from Tone at the Top to Checks and Balances

For several decades, governance experts focused on improving the tone at the top. Experts believed a strong CEO setting the right tone was the best way to ensure good management practices and adequate controls. However, a distinct shift is solidly under way now, focused on improved checks and balances among fundamental elements of organization governance: the board, the board committees, and senior management in which the corporate governance lawyer occupies an important role.

The checks and balances approach addresses the roles, responsibilities, and relationships among various elements of the governance process. This shift is permanent, and deep-seated forces drive it. Institutional investors, individual investors, and other market and regulatory interests increasingly demand those participants in organizational governance recognize their responsibilities, are held accountable in addressing these responsibilities, and understand their role is one of service rather than entitlement.

Not long ago, senior management preferred, and often secured, limited involvement. Even when outside directors were on boards, typically they were not selected for their managerial or technical skills. Instead, these board members frequently focused on the prestige of their role, rather than the performance of their responsibilities.

Awareness of this governance deficiency is longstanding. To repeat what has been said earlier, Courtney Brown, former dean of the College of Business at Columbia and a board member of several well-known companies, confirmed this deficiency in the preface of his 1976 book Putting Corporate Boards to Work:

> Members of governing boards have a prestigious status in society—more prestigious than the present nature of their activities can support. It is a status that reflects the popular belief and expectation that governing boards do indeed govern. Building on this preconception, the work of governing

boards can and should be clarified and strengthened to the ultimate benefit of corporations and society.[8]

Nonetheless, despite the efforts of Brown and others, attempts at improving organization governance continued to focus on improving the tone at the top, stressing the need for improved character, integrity, and responsibility primarily on the part of senior management.

A. The Tide Begins to Turn

In the late 1990s, Arthur Levitt, then the Chair of the Securities and Exchange Commission, spoke thoughtfully and firmly about the need for checks and balances in financial reporting. Early in 1998, he expressed concerns about selective disclosure of firm information. On September 28, 1998, speaking at the NYU Center for Law and Business, Levitt spoke of his concerns regarding earnings management, and other issues. Importantly, he pointed to the need for checks and balances to be put in place to address a range of issues.

Levitt referred to his early 1998 remarks saying:

Seven months ago, I expressed concerns about selective disclosure. Through conference calls or embargoed press releases, analysts and institutional investors often hear about material news before it is made public. In the interval, there is a great deal of unusual trading. The practice had been going on for a long time. And, while everyone was aware of it, and most were extremely uncomfortable with it, few spoke out. As the investor's advocate, the SEC did and we will continue to do so.

Levitt then turned to earnings management:

Increasingly, I have become concerned that the motivation to meet Wall Street earnings expectations may be overriding common sense business practices. Too many corporate managers, auditors, and analysts are participants in a game of nods and winks. In the zeal to satisfy consensus earnings estimates and project a smooth earnings path, wishful thinking may be winning the day over faithful representation.

As a result, I fear that we are witnessing an erosion in the quality of earnings, and therefore, the quality of financial reporting. Managing may be giving way to manipulation; Integrity may be losing out to illusion.

Many in corporate America are just as frustrated and concerned about this trend as we, at the SEC, are. They know how difficult it is to hold the line on

[8] Brown is sited not because he was the only one calling attention to the issues, but because he did not allow the prestige of these positions he held to distract him from the reality of what was occurring.

good practices when their competitors operate in the gray area between legitimacy and outright fraud.

A gray area where the accounting is being perverted; where managers are cutting corners; and, where earnings reports reflect the desires of management rather than the underlying financial performance of the company.

Levitt opened his remarks saying:

Tonight, I want to talk about why integrity in financial reporting is under stress and explore five of the more common accounting gimmicks we've been seeing. Finally, I will outline a framework for a financial community response to this situation.

This necessary response involves improving both our accounting and disclosure rules, as well as the oversight and function of outside auditors and board audit committees. I am also calling upon a broad spectrum of capital market participants, from corporate management to Wall Street analysts to investors, to stand together and re-energize the touchstone of our financial reporting system: transparency and comparability.

This is a financial community problem. It can't be solved by a government mandate: it demands a financial community response.

Here, when he discusses "a framework for a financial community response to this situation," he is focused on creating a set of checks and balances to address the financial community problem that he recognizes cannot be solved by a government mandate but, instead, demands a financial community response.

He discusses the pressure to "make your numbers"; "big bath" restructuring charges; creative acquisition accounting; miscellaneous "cookie jar reserves," "materiality"; and "revenue recognition."

He then discusses creating an action plan: improving the accounting framework, which involved the SEC staff, the accounting profession and firms themselves addressing purchased R&D, changes in accounting assumptions, restructurings, large acquisition write-offs, and revenue recognition.

He then shifted focus to checks and balances, advocating for private sector standard setters to take action where current standards and guidance are inadequate. He highlighted the role of SEC review and enforcement teams in reinforcing regulatory initiatives, specifically targeting reviews of public company announcements, write-offs, and other practices. He called for improved outside auditing in the financial reporting process, pointing to recent headlines of accounting failures that questioned the thoroughness of audits. He noted that the auditors are the public's watchdog in the financial reporting process, and the integrity of that information must take precedence over any desire for cost efficiencies or competitive advantage in the audit process. Additionally, he mentioned his proposal for the Public Oversight Board to establish a group of all the major constituencies to review the performance of audits and related issues.

Also, he called for strengthening the audit committee process stating "qualified, committed, independent and tough-mined audit committees represent the most reliable guardians of the public interest." Additionally, he emphasized that committee members must have a financial background, with no ties to the chairman or the company; where they have their own advisers, ask tough questions of management and outside auditors—with ultimately the investor interest being served.

Levitt continued:

As part eight of this comprehensive effort to address earnings management, the New York Stock Exchange and the National Association of Securities Dealers have agreed to sponsor a "blue- ribbon" panel to be headed by John Whitehead, former Deputy Secretary of State and retired senior partner of Goldman, Sachs, and Ira Millstein, a lawyer and noted corporate governance expert. Within the next 90 days, this distinguished group will develop a series of far-ranging recommendations intended to empower audit committees to function as the ultimate guardian of investor interests and corporate accountability. They are going to examine how we can get the right people to do the right things and ask the right questions.

He concluded with a call for a cultural change:

Finally, I'm challenging corporate management and Wall Street to reexamine our current environment. I believe we need to embrace nothing less than a cultural change. For corporate managers, remember, the integrity of the numbers in the financial reporting system is directly related to the long-term interests of a corporation. While the temptations are great, and the pressures strong, illusions in numbers are only that—ephemeral, and ultimately self-destructive.

Levitt, throughout his remarks, focused on putting effective checks and balances in place in every aspect of the financial reporting process. He made no mention of focusing on tone at the top. Instead, the multiple checks and balances needed to be established and positioned to insure the processes. Levitt turned on the light. The multiple checks and balances needed in the financial reporting process would soon be required across the company.

B. Shifting Focus from Tone at the Top

Only a few years later, one of the authors of this book and four other senior executives hit the issue head on. They recognized a fundamental shift was underway, and there was growing recognition that a structure of checks and balances was needed, characterized by transparency. These executives understood a focus solely on tone at the top would continue to lead to periodic organization collapses and significant damages. Three were currently directors of large public firms, a fourth had held board positions and served as managing director of large general partnerships, and the fifth had been a senior executive of a large public-private entity. Their recognition of this shift was supported by the executive director of the New York State Society of CPAs and by the editor of the "The CPA Journal," where their writing was published.[9] Both the executive director and the editor believed the intensified level of interest in improved organization governance and the shift toward improving checks and balances were permanent.

In both advisory and litigation capacities, it is apparent that the courts, institutional investors, individual investors, insurers, and the plaintiffs' bar are focused on the requirement that each element of the corporate governance process recognize and fulfill its respective responsibilities. The sizable settlements in recent high-profile litigation confirm this. These settlements continue to grow in both monetary amounts and the responsibilities of boards.

Institutional investors have urged all of the involved parties to recognize their responsibilities. Joining this call are individual investors, a growing number of whom are directly responsible for managing their savings and retirement benefits. Insurers have seen directors' and officers' insurance lines incur significant losses. These insurers are not only looking at significant premium adjustments, but also implementing co-insurance solutions. Hard markets in terms of insurance premiums come and go as the competition may warrant. However, whether pricing is hard or soft, D&O insurers are increasingly concerned with how a company conducts its corporate governance.

Up until about mid-2022, the D&O insurance market was hard, i.e., premiums were relatively high and policy terms and conditions were restrictive at times. Increased competition among insurers subsequently softened the market in terms of pricing, but the insurance underwriters have remained highly interested in corporate governance, particularly concerning cybersecurity. *Bingle/SolarWinds* is perceived by many insurers as a close call that easily could have gone the other way. Therefore, anticipate D&O insurers to do vigorous due diligence on a company's controls that would enable them to successfully defend a *Caremark* claim. Expect to see both insurers and insured corporations engage with outside experts to help with this due diligence and ensure that the underwriting of these risks is tested vigorously.

The five authors believe the shift in the focus of organization governance to an improved set of checks and balances is a win-win situation for all involved.

[9] "From 'Tone at the Top' To 'Checks and Balances,'" H. Stephen Grace, Jr. co-authored with James N. Clark, R. Hartwell Gardner, John E. Haupert and Robert S. Roath, "*The CPA Journal*," March 2002, p. 63. Lou Grumet was the Executive Director of NYSSCPA, and Bob Colson was he Editor of the "The CPA Journal."

Organization governance is not a zero-sum game, nor are its structure and operation. This is not about shifting power from one participant in the governance process to another. An improved set of checks and balances entails the dynamic definition of the roles and responsibilities of every participant in a manner that optimizes potential synergies. Governance is a win-win or a lose-lose situation—not only for the participants, but for all of society.

The authors recognized that the emphasis on tone at the top overlooked history. They noted that experience had demonstrated that governing structures that consolidate power and authority into fewer hands, while conceptually attractive for potential efficiency and effectiveness, consistently fell short of these conceptual ideals. Lord Acton told us long ago, "Power tends to corrupt, and absolute power corrupts absolutely." Dictatorships and monarchies dominate the history of political governance, although they have consistently failed. These failures led to the evolution of a democratic form of government, which, despite its seemingly time-consuming checks and balances, has proven to be the most effective form of government.

The authors pointed out that the shift to an improved set of checks and balances in organization governance is underway. Each of the key elements of the organization governance structure—the board, the board committees, and senior management—must closely examine their roles, responsibilities, and relationships with the other elements of the organization governance structure. From their perspective, ultimate accountability should rest with senior management, the board, and board committees, and those roles and relationships must be defined clearly and understood in that context. The board, working with its board committees, must accept the ultimate responsibility for ensuring the quality and integrity of the risk and control environment within their responsibilities for the governance, oversight, and management of the organization. Integral to the checks and balances is the corporate governance lawyer, who plays a role in determining the required checks and balances. On behalf of their corporate client, corporate governance lawyers monitor the appropriateness of the checks and balances in place and under development.

C. Paul Volcker and Arthur Levitt on Checks and Balances

Writing in *The Wall Street Journal* in 2004, Volcker and Levitt were direct on the need for checks and balances:

> Two years ago this summer, Congress passed the Sarbanes-Oxley Act, the most far-reaching corporate reform legislation in 60 years, with the support of all but three members of Congress who voted. *It was a moment of rare bipartisan action in response to the breakdown in corporate checks and*

balances that cost investors hundreds of billions of dollars in losses. (Note that no mention was made of tone at the top.)

Volcker and Levitt pointed out:

> Measures to reform the auditing profession and to assure its independence were central elements of the new legislation. Complementing them were strong new corporate governance rules ranging from who can sit on their boards and audit committees to new and clear responsibilities for internal controls and the accuracy of financial reports. These reforms were long overdue, and have made companies more transparent and accountable to shareholders.

Volcker and Levitt continued, discussing the ongoing controversy of whether Sarbanes-Oxley went too far in terms of required compliance and associated upfront and ongoing cost: They explained that there is a reason why the upfront costs are so expensive:

> For too long, too many companies have lacked adequate internal controls. Despite legislation existing for over a quarter of a century mandating that companies have adequate internal controls, in recent years investors have had to watch as more than a thousand public companies issued corrections for errors in their financial statements. In 2003 alone, fifty-seven large and small companies reported material weaknesses in their controls once their auditors were terminated. And auditors who used to test all the controls on which they were relying annually, cut back on the level of their tests significantly as they faced pressures to reduce their fees. The investing public had no idea of the impending disaster, and with no one looking, lines were allowed to be crossed.

From the perspective of Volcker and Levitt:

> Five million dollars down and $1.5 million a year is not too much to pay for a multibillion-dollar international company when compared to how much investors have lost—and stand to lose—if internal controls are not improved. Put it in the context of the tens of millions of dollars paid to investment bankers to advise on a deal, or on legal fees when things go wrong—or think of the $90 billion investors lost just on the collapse of Enron alone. By that calculus, Sarbanes-Oxley clearly meets the cost-benefit test and is worth every penny.

In their conclusion, Volcker and Levitt returned to the need for and effectiveness of checks and balances:

> Becoming a public company opens up a world of opportunity for a firm, but with that comes a responsibility to its shareholders. For too many years, too

many people in and around our markets were shirking that responsibility, and shareholders suffered through investments made on bad information, restatements, and bankruptcies. Sarbanes-Oxley was passed to reinforce the duties that directors, executives, auditors, and others have to the investing public. It seeks to bring accountability back into the boardroom and executive suites.

They concluded:

> While there are direct money costs involved in compliance, we believe that an investment in good corporate governance, professional integrity and transparency will pay dividends in the form of investor confidence, more efficient markets, and more market participation for years to come. Volcker and Levitt's remarks represent a clear stepping away from the concept of "tone at the top" being the proper governance focus. The concept is simply omitted from their thoughts and recommendations.

D. Board Oversight and Governance: From Tone at the Top to Substantive Checks and Balances

The evolution from tone at the top to checks and balances continues. Following the well-publicized control breakdowns at Wells Fargo Bank and Boeing, coupled with regulatory actions, boards of directors of public companies and financial institutions have faced increased scrutiny and have been directed to improve oversight and enhance corporate governance. Responding to these demands from regulators and shareholders to improve board oversight and governance, boards are evolving from an approach of focusing primarily on tone at the top and shifting to implementation of substantive checks and balances. There is also a growing emphasis on and considering broader aspects of ethics, values, and corporate culture.

During this shift, boards must not only oversee checks and balances being put in place, but also may assume direct responsibilities regarding the design of the checks and balances, particularly those related to the CEO and other members of senior management. Because several reported ethics problems and failures in corporate controls have involved the senior-most executives, more of the responsibility for addressing these risks will fall to a company's board. Typically, the board will involve internal and external corporate governance lawyers in these matters.

Wells Fargo and Boeing address the integration of board oversight and governance responsibilities, along with what we continue to observe as the evolution from a focus on tone at the top to a focus on checks and balances. Wells Fargo and Boeing also address the importance of ethics and values in corporate culture within the context of board governance.

1. Mandating Improved Board Oversight and Governance—Wells Fargo

On February 2, 2018, the U.S. Federal Reserve Board announced consent and cease-and-desist orders requiring improvements in Wells Fargo Bank's governance, risk management processes, controls, and board oversight. This was prompted by widespread abuses in consumer sales practices and control breakdowns that occurred over several years. The orders included a growth restriction on the company until sufficient improvements were implemented. Both the Federal Reserve Board and Wells Fargo confirmed the need for improvement, stating, "Within sixty days the company's board will submit a plan to further enhance the board's effectiveness in carrying out its oversight and governance of the company." This followed the board's submission of plans for governance and for oversight that the Fed deemed as inadequate. The Fed mandated the plans be revised and mandated that two third-party consultants review the revised plans, and stipulated the entire process be completed within sixty days.

In a press release, the Fed also criticized the job performance of Wells Fargo's board and CEO, stating that the Fed, "has sent letters to each current Wells Fargo board member confirming that the firm's board of directors during the period of compliance breakdowns did not meet supervisory expectations. Letters were also sent to former Chairman and Chief Executive Officer John Stumpf and past lead independent director Steven Sanger stating that their performance in those roles, in particular, did not meet the Federal Reserve's expectations."

The Fed's regulatory action expanded what many individuals and organizations traditionally considered a customary and general oversight responsibility. Instead, it transformed this oversight duty into a mandated obligation to institute procedures for enhanced oversight and governance. The requirement for reporting on enhanced oversight and governance measures represented a significant step. However, as we've mentioned throughout this book, the view that a fundamental responsibility of a governing board is to govern is not a new perspective. As mentioned earlier, retired Delaware Supreme Court Chief Justice E. Norman Veasey, in his May 2005[10] *Pennsylvania Law Review* article, stated stockholders should have the right to expect that, "the board of directors will actually direct and monitor the management of the company, including strategic business and fundamental structural changes." Furthermore, the idea that directors have management as well as oversight responsibilities was stated earlier in a quote from retired Delaware Chancery Court Chancellor William B. Chandler, in his opinion in the 2003 Disney shareowner derivative suit.

[10] Veasey, What Happened in Delaware Corporate Law and Governance from 1992–2004. 155 University of Pennsylvania Law Review 5, May 2005.

As mentioned earlier on the Federal Reserve's website, the Fed describes a board's responsibility to create and enforce prudent policies and practices with the following statement: "Directors are placed in a position of trust by the bank's shareholders, and both statutes and common law place responsibility for the affairs of a bank firmly and squarely on the board of directors. The board of directors of a bank should delegate the day-to-day routine of conducting the bank's business to its officers and employees, but the board cannot delegate its responsibility for the consequences of unsound or imprudent policies and practices." In direct terms, boards must govern and oversight and, if necessary, manage the organization.[11]

Boards that want to address the expectations for enhanced oversight and governance face many challenges, among them a lack of definition of what constitutes effective governance in organizations. Economists have long recognized that the division of labor of a firm is specific to a firm at a point in time. As such, there is no single standard and no single metric for what constitutes effective governance—there is no common best practice, no one-size-fits-all approach to follow. Just as the division of labor in an organization is unique to each organization and to each point in time, effective governance is both organization specific and time specific. Models and practices are useful resources to consult when designing governance and control structures, but there is no off-the-shelf, single best way for any organization. An organization's needs inevitably will change over time, sometimes unexpectedly and rapidly in response to a crisis or other circumstances. The corporate governance lawyer plays an important role in examining whether the designed and implemented governance measures align with the firm's requirements in the context of the lawyer's responsibilities, and the lawyer's assistance to the board.

The "Principles of Corporate Governance," issued by the Business Roundtable (BRT), which is an organization of CEOs from America's top companies, is a well-respected document that speaks to this reality. The following is a short excerpt from the update of Principles of Corporate Governance, issued in 2016.

> In light of the evolving landscape affecting U.S. public companies, Business Roundtable has updated Principles of Corporate Governance. Although Business Roundtable believes that these principles represent current practical and effective corporate governance practices, it recognizes that wide variations exist among the businesses, relevant regulatory regimes, ownership structures and investors of U.S. public companies. No one approach to corporate governance may be right for all companies, and Business

[11] The discussion of the economics of ownership and the evolution of board and board committee responsibilities in chapter I further confirms these responsibilities.

> Roundtable does not prescribe or endorse any particular option, leaving that to the considered judgment of boards, management and shareholders. Accordingly, each company should look to these principles as a guide in developing the structures, practices and processes that are appropriate in light of its needs and circumstances.

The BRT's principles, along with other corporate governance references, underscore the importance of each company's senior management and board of directors dedicating time and attention to designing structures, policies, and processes to provide effective governance in their organization's unique situation. Also, it is important to examine and evaluate governance on an ongoing basis, especially as special events and circumstances arise. Mergers, acquisitions, takeover attempts, product failures, breakdowns in controls, lapses in ethical conduct—all of these and additional special circumstances can come up at any time. The corporate governance lawyer's ongoing role of participating in insuring what is required at that time and place is being increasingly recognized.

There is a wide range of structures, functions, and players involved in considering a company's governance and control system, as illustrated earlier in Figure 2. Figure 2 sets out the breadth of relationships that the board must address when formulating and implementing effective corporate governance practices. Once addressed, these relationships require monitoring and updating. As is apparent in Figure 2, the corporate governance lawyer's involvement often will be in multiple areas.

2. Evolving From Tone at the Top to Checks and Balances

To emphasize again, for the past several decades, corporate governance experts focused on an approach of improving the tone at the top with the belief that a strong CEO establishing the right tone was the most effective way to ensure sound management practices and adequate controls throughout a company. However, as failures occurred, sometimes involving CEOs who had ostensibly set the right tone in statements to employees and the public, the limitations of this reliance became evident. A distinct shift in approach is underway, focusing now on a substantive set of checks and balances as essential in carrying out effective governance.

Proper implementation of substantive checks and balances addresses the roles, responsibilities, and relationships among the key elements and players in a firm's governance, controls, and oversight system. As mentioned earlier, there is a growing demand from institutional investors, individual investors, and other market and regulatory interests for those involved in corporate governance to recognize and be held accountable for addressing these responsibilities.

Another emerging expectation is that senior leaders in an organization, both board and management, recognize that a leader's role is one of service rather than entitlement. Experience has demonstrated that governing structures that consolidate power and authority into fewer hands, although conceptually attractive in terms of potential efficiency and effectiveness, frequently fail to meet conceptual ideals if those in power feel entitled to do what they want. Without effective oversight and a system of checks and balances, conditions are ripe for misconduct. In response to this reality, boards cannot simply witness the implementation of the checks and balances, but also, they must become involved in formulating the checks and balances and occupy active roles in the execution therein. Carrying out these active roles will lead to regular interaction with the CEO, CFO, CLO, and others in senior management as well as with a company's internal and external auditors. While tone at the top may sometimes seem to be words that do not actually affect behavior, the institution of checks and balances can exert considerable influence.

A careful inspection of the factors that underly the effectiveness of successful organizations indicates that, over time, they have implemented highly effective policies, procedures, and controls. Individuals have well-defined responsibilities; the organizations make certain that individuals understand those responsibilities, and the organizations demand strict accountability. Individuals must understand the organization's mission and values and have an attitude of service. Furthermore, there are well-understood consequences for falling short in discharging responsibilities, creating a clear measure of accountability.

3. Effective Governance Includes Ethics, Values, and Corporate Culture

In addition to the structures, policies, and processes that provide checks and balances, effective governance includes an organization's ethics, values, and corporate culture. Many problems in recent years have involved CEOs and others in senior management. Typically, board members have not been involved, but it has occurred. Ethics issues can arise at any level. However, most corporate efforts addressing ethical issues have been developed for the entire organization, but with limited attention being paid specifically to those in upper management.

There are good business reasons to consider implementing ethics programs for senior leaders—programs that are based on long-standing principles and that boards implement for themselves and senior management. In this approach, the board would create a program and set expectations, then continue to monitor and periodically review the program, modifying appropriately as needed. Such programs integrate oversight and governance with ethics, values, and corporate culture in a way that can enhance success of an organization.

A successful organization is appealing to prospective employees who will serve as its intellectual capital. It is an increasing popular belief that a firm's most valuable asset is its intellectual capital. The recognition and value placed on intellectual capital are evident when observing the emergence and growth of innovative firms such as Google and Apple. Although it can be difficult to measure, intellectual capital is credited with significant economic productivity increases and can play a critical role in the achievement and continuation of profitability in organizations. However, beyond the issues of profitability and monetary returns traditional financial capital providers and the owners of the physical components of production have sought, the intellectual capital owners—the skilled individuals who are today's professionals—typically seek to maximize their economic wellbeing with a combination of monetary and non-monetary compensation. Economic well-being is a broad concept that encompasses various factors affecting the overall quality of life, instead of financial well-being, which considers only monetary compensation and the accumulation of wealth. One component of non-monetary compensation that interests many professionals today is a management culture based on ethics and values and respect, one that incorporates an attitude of responsibility, accountability, and service, as well as expertise and performance excellence.

The most effective managers of today's intellectual capital and professionals will be those who demonstrate a sense of responsibility, a willingness to be accountable, and an attitude of service. Many professionals now tend to believe that doing well and doing good are not mutually exclusive, and that a combination of the two will result in the maximization of their individual economic well-being. Boards and management leaders who understand the difference between economic and financial well-being and the complementary relationship between doing well and doing good are more prone to success. In contrast, management scenarios that are structured around entitlement or privilege are not likely to be tolerated or sustainable. Intellectual capital is highly mobile, and those individuals providing that capital can exercise that mobility if management is not clear in its recognition of responsibilities, accountability, and an attitude of service.

Robert Fogel, who we mentioned earlier, discussed profound long-term trends in individual work habits in his book, *The Fourth Great Awakening: The Future of Egalitarianism in America* (2000). He notes that over the last 100 years there has been a considerable reduction in the time individuals spend in earnwork—that is, work associated with earning wages which in turn permits the acquisition of material possessions. He points out that what has increased is the time individuals spend in volwork—that is, personal time directed toward what he calls non-material and spiritual goods. Fogel found that individuals have consciously and deliberately made the decision to reduce the amount of earnwork and, thus, the material possessions they might otherwise acquire. Instead, they choose to devote their time to family, community, religious, and other related activities. Fogel's analysis underscores an important lesson for management: Individuals seek to maximize not only their financial wealth, but also their personal utility and personal satisfaction. They become more cognizant of the activities that contribute to their economic well-being. They see many more options and alternatives available to help them to achieve an increased level of economic well-being. The pandemic has evidenced this awareness and the associated drive, in terms of the relocations—both locational and employment-wise—that have occurred.

Today's professionals expect management to have a comprehensive understanding of and a willingness to address responsibilities. They expect management to be accountable, and to implement appropriate sets of checks and balances for their own activities, which will ensure accountability on the part of all the involved parties. Most importantly, they want management to bring an attitude of service to leadership. Smart, well-trained, and mobile, today's professionals will gravitate to working environments where management respects them. The need for management to demonstrate an attitude of service is not surprising. An attitude of service is a shared quality among the most widely respected and notable leaders from all walks of life. A continuation of the discussion of these issues occurs in chapter VII.

4. Improving Oversight and Governance Is Timely and Good Business

In the interest of achieving and maintaining effective oversight and governance, and to earn the respect and loyalty of workers, boards should focus on management's ethics, as well as the traditional focus on the organization's ethics. It is timely and good business for boards to continue to implement and update systems of substantive checks and balances that start with the CEO, senior management, and the board itself, and then proceed through the entire organization. Improving board and organizational oversight and governance will not only lower the risk of failures and problems in the organization, but also it can bring sustainable operating benefits to a company and its shareholders.

E. Boeing and the Ongoing Evolution of Director Responsibilities

The metaphorical "governance bells" continue to ring for corporate, non-corporate, not-for-profit, governmental, and other organizations. The increasing focus on director responsibilities for effective governance is being driven by investors, other stakeholders, regulators, insurance carriers, and growing litigation risk. The focus on board governance, oversight, and management responsibilities point to the need to ensure substantive checks and balances exist and to explore opportunities to create governance structures with a harder edge. These structures can help ensure proper communication and operational interaction between the board, management, and others. Again, a corporate governance lawyer contributes to insuring the existence of these structures.

A review of the Boeing Company Derivative litigation demonstrates the increased focus on director responsibilities. An analysis of Delaware Vice

Chancellor Zurn's September 7, 2021, MEMORANDUM OPINION and her findings regarding director failures initiates the review. Then, we identify and address these fundamental governance breakdowns.

1. In Re The Boeing Company Derivative Litigation, Court of Chancery, State of Delaware, C.A. No. 2019-0907-MTZ, *Decided* September 7, 2021

Vice Chancellor Zurn states in this opinion:

> The narrow question before this Court today is whether Boeing's stockholders have alleged that a majority of the Company's directors face a substantial likelihood of liability for Boeing's losses. This may be based on the directors' complete failure to establish a reporting system for airplane safety, or their turning a blind eye to a red flag representing airplane safety problems. I conclude the stockholders have pled both sources of board liability. The stockholders may pursue the Company's oversight claim against the board.

In her opinion, the vice chancellor stated, "The Board publicly lied about if and how it monitored the 737 Max's safety." The Opinion cites 2019 interviews of the Board's Lead Director, David Calhoun, who became Boeing's CEO in January 2020, and certain representations he made regarding the Lion Air crash and the Ethiopian Airlines crash. The vice chancellor's Opinion states, "Each of Calhoun's representations was false."

Shortly after the Opinion was issued, Boeing's CEO and other current and former directors asked the vice chancellor to clarify her legal opinion where she found the Board "publicly lied." Those defendants moved to settle the case. However, the finding that they "publicly lied" is a gray area to be addressed on multiple fronts within and outside of litigation.

2. Identifying and Addressing Fundamental Governance Breakdowns

The vice chancellor's finding of "the director's complete failure to establish a reporting system for airplane safety" and her finding that "their turning a blind eye to a red flag representing airplane safety problems" are indicative of a board operating in an tone at the top framework where the CEO may direct or dictate to the board. As we mentioned previously, a governance structure that incorporates transparency and "substantive checks and balances"[12] is required versus a tone at the top approach. This is not a new concept. Members of the Grace & Co. board of advisors and other experienced business decision makers addressed it years

[12] *Ibid.*, 63.

ago.[13] Yet, a board's perception of its role as only that of oversight, and at times limited oversight, persists on many boards, often with the support or influence of the CEO.

Often, boards, with the assistance of the corporate governance lawyers, can use internal resources to ensure the boards have access to that information necessary to address their responsibilities. In chapter V, we discuss the value of these internal resources to boards and recognize that boards also can call on external resources.[14]

Under the $237.5 million agreement to settle the litigation, Boeing's board added a director with safety experience and adopted other internal measures. Boeing agreed to ensure that at least three directors have such expertise. The relationship between those new board members and possibly other board members and management is an ongoing interactive relationship where the company can draw on the talents and experience of those board members.

An example of board members participating in addressing management responsibilities arose when Michael Eisner, former CEO of Walt Disney, utilized the chairman of Disney's compensation committee and another experienced director to handle the employment negotiations with Michael Ovitz and his advisers.[15] An interactive relationship between certain directors and members of management helps ensure the quality of the flow of information both to and from the board, and is demonstrative of the nature of the working relationships/checks and balances between the board and management that can be developed.

3. The Economics of Organization Governance

The economics of organization governance point to the responsibilities of ownership and its agents for the governance, oversight, and management of the organization. The board of directors, as owners or agents for ownership, bear the responsibility for the governance, oversight, and management of the organization. The Boeing litigation demonstrates the increased focus on these fundamental director responsibilities.

---

[13] *Ibid.*, 63.

[14] Board Oversight and Governance: From Tone at the Top to Substantive Checks and Balances," by H. Stephen Grace, Jr., S. Lawrence Prendergast, and Susan Koski-Grafer, *Business Law Today*, February 2019.

[15] H. Stephen Grace, Jr. "An Insider Revisits the 'Disney Case,'" *Directors Monthly*, August 2008, pp. 1, 3–6. H. Stephen Grace, Jr. "Plaintiff Expert Reports: An Insider Revisits Disney," *New York State Bar Association Journal*, July/August 2009, pp. 24–29. H. Stephen Grace, Jr. "Governance Lessons from the Disney Litigation, "co-authored with John E. Haupert, ABA's Business Law Today, September 2011. H. Stephen Grace, Jr. "Corporate Governance: Lessons From Life and Litigation—With Implications for Corporate Counsel," co-authored with John E. Haupert, *New York State Bar Association Journal*, March/April 2013.

IV. Why a Company Should Consider Using an Executive Committee of its Board of Directors

This chapter title is not meant to indicate that a firm should use an executive committee. Instead, the chapter title calls for the consideration of an executive committee of its board of directors. Why? In brief:

1. In organizations of all sizes, board meetings occur only on a periodic basis, which can make it challenging for boards to meet their obligations.
2. The creation of an executive committee can improve the flow of information that assists an organization's management and board in governing effectively, and
3. An enhanced ability to monitor and consult can help an organization's CEO, board of directors, and general counsel/chief legal officer and others carry out effective corporate governance.

The role of a public corporation's in-house general counsel/chief legal officer has always been a difficult balancing act. General counsel must be an expert advisor to the company's CEO and board of directors. General counsel must fulfill significant legal obligations to the company's owners and creditors. Also, an effective general counsel must function as a knowledgeable business partner in senior management. The complex responsibilities of the position have been covered extensively in many professional publications and have been amplified by laws passed, regulations issued, and court cases over many years.[16]

[16] See E. Norman Veasey & Christine T. Di Guglielmo, Indispensable Counsel (Oxford University Press, 2012) (a comprehensive description of the responsibilities and obligations of counsel, the relevant legal environment, and numerous experiences of job incumbents).

The obligations of boards of directors to monitor, oversee, and direct the affairs of a public corporation have a similar level of complexity. In companies of all sizes, having only periodic board meetings can make it challenging to meet these obligations. To fulfill governance responsibilities, a board must understand and address issues and developments that can arise in the organization at any time.

Because management is a continuous process and board processes are intermittent, creating an executive committee can improve the information flow to help the organization's management and board govern effectively. Providing relevant and timely information is a critical aspect of the checks and balances systems in managing and directing company affairs.

A. What Is a Board Executive Committee?

Typically, public company boards of directors have three standing committees that are mandated by regulators and listing exchanges: an audit committee, a nominating and governance committee, and a compensation committee. The responsibilities of these standing committees are described and discussed in a company's public disclosures. Financial institutions also are mandated to have a committee that addresses risk. Other organizations often follow this structure. However, just as financial institutions have additional committees, each organization must consider what is necessary for the board to address its governance, oversight, and management responsibilities.

Over time, companies have established other committees of the board to specialize in such matters as technology, risk identification and management, safety and security, environmental issues, human capital, and other areas. Some companies have created an executive committee to address matters that may need monitoring and attention between regularly scheduled board meetings. The roles of these executive committees can vary among companies and with changing circumstances within a company. One company describes its executive committee in its annual report as follows:

> Executive Committee (three directors) is to, as more fully specified herein, (1) monitor and review the operations of the Company and its subsidiaries (collectively, the Group), (2) exercise specific delegated powers of the Board, (3) review and provide recommendations on matters that would require the approval of the Board and (4) exercise such other powers and responsibilities as may be delegated to the Committee by the Board from time to time consistent with the Company's Amended and Restated Certificate of Incorporation (the Certificate) and Amended and Restated Bylaws (the Bylaws), within the parameters delegated by the Board. The Committee shall meet as and when any member of the Committee deems necessary or

desirable, subject to notice (or waiver of notice) being given in accordance with the rules and procedures of the Committee.[17]

Charters for executive committees may also describe specific limitations on committee activities. Information about a company's board committees and board committee charters can generally be obtained from annual reports, proxy statements, or upon request to a company's investor relations organization. This information can be useful to organizations that want to examine their governance structure.

B. Three Reasons for a Company to Consider the Use of an Executive Committee

1. An executive committee serves as a valuable resource for monitoring a wide range of developments on an ongoing basis. By eliminating the need for periodic meetings with fixed schedules or travel, and leveraging technology, such a committee can stay aware of internal and external developments affecting the business and can act whenever such matters arise. The committee can be on the lookout for issues that warrant consultation and discussion among the CEO, CFO, general counsel, and other senior management.
2. An executive committee can serve as a sounding board for the general counsel and CEO, other members of senior management, and independent directors to explore emerging issues or concerns that don't require a presentation to the full board. Having a small, knowledgeable group that the CEO and general counsel can consult with can facilitate preliminary evaluation of an issue and provide practical and useful advice. It allows issues to be discussed and evaluated and in some cases, potentially resolved, before they need to be added to a board's agenda. Preliminary evaluation also facilitates definition and preparation of matters that do move on to the board.
3. The effectiveness of a company's corporate governance—its system of governing the corporation—is dependent on creating the right checks and balances and information flows. A small executive committee can institute flexible and efficient information processes that start, stop, and change easily as needed.
4. Executive committee access to inside-the-company sources, with an ability to inquire about matters as needed, can strengthen the checks and balances in the corporation. Better communications and stronger information

[17] BOE Annual Report 2019, at www.cboe.com.

flows at early stages might have helped avoid the widespread and highly publicized control breakdowns that occurred at Enron,[18] WorldCom,[19] and more recently at Wells Fargo.[20] In these cases, massive reputational and financial damage was done.

C. Some Caveats for Creating and Using an Executive Committee

It is important to distinguish between monitor, discuss, and advise versus make decisions. When creating an executive committee, a company must not create an undesirable two-tier power dynamic inside the board. Meaning, the executive committee should not take on decision-making authority that, under the bylaws, belongs with the full board. To minimize this risk, the committee should have a well-defined charter with clearly described delegations, along with its own internal set of checks and balances.

An executive committee's processes for information gathering should be relevant, timely, and efficient, as well as cognizant of the need to avoid placing unnecessary burdens on management. Similarly, reporting to the full board should be efficient, with written summaries to reduce time spent on routine matters in periodic board meetings.

An executive committee should be small, generally not more than three to five people, including the CEO. It should include two independent directors who have relevant experience and business knowledge. The governance structure is specific to a firm at a given point in time, and the use of an executive committee will vary within a firm as well as between firms.

An executive committee opens the door to in-depth, ongoing discussions with the corporate governance lawyer. Board members on the executive committee can drill into legal and legally related operating issues being addressed by the company. Concerns of the lawyer can be identified and discussed, while steps are put in place when needed. However, this type of discussion is unlikely to occur at a board meeting. These same advantages cross into the activities of the CFO and others, surfacing a range of issues that may require the type of attention that may not be available at the board meetings. The establishment and operation of an executive committee is an effective channel for the corporate governance lawyer to keep the board informed of legal and related developments, as well as position the corporate governance lawyer to address their role as an important element of the necessary checks and balances for the firm.

---

[18] See In *re Enron Corp. Sec. Litig.*, 586 F. Supp. 2d 732, 789 (S.D. Tex. 2008).

[19] See In *re WorldCom, Inc. Sec. Litig.*, 346 F. Supp. 2d 628 (S.D.N.Y. 2004).

[20] *In re Wells Fargo & Company Securities Litigation*, Case No. 1:20-cv-04494-GHW, United States District Court, Southern District of New York.

V. Organization Governance and Information Gaps: Importance of Internal Reporting and Internal Information for Board Oversight

The existence and responsibilities of specialized committees on boards of directors have evolved and will continue to evolve. Questions arise regarding whether boards are receiving and utilizing adequate information and support. Courts and eminent legal authorities have emphasized repeatedly the significant responsibilities of boards' organization governance, and for oversight of the management of organizations, whether they are public companies or otherwise. The corporate governance lawyer is in the middle of this. Typically, the lawyer is not responsible for making these committees function effectively, but they have a responsibility for ensuring the committees are functioning properly. This chapter addresses the responsibilities and information requirements and can be shared with boards and management.

A. Introduction

The evolution of organization governance and board of directors' responsibilities is continuing. Recent actions of shareowner activist groups and securities regulators—and reports of shareowner votes in corporate annual meetings—provide many indications of ongoing growth in public expectations for the roles and performance of boards of directors.

As mentioned earlier, the existence and responsibilities of specialized committees on boards of directors continue to evolve. In addition to long-established types of board committees such as the audit, finance, compensation, risk management, and nominating and governance committees, we now see committees being formed to address such issues as science, technology, and innovation, cybersecurity, health, safety and security, environment, and sustainability, along with other concerns. While these topics are all valid considerations, one wonders how many committees one board of directors can administer and support effectively. And how can numerous board committees successfully monitor organizational issues and developments and then report on these matters in periodic board meetings? The corporate governance lawyer is obligated to understand the roles and responsibilities of these committees and simultaneously monitor their ongoing activities.

With these growing expectations, further questions arise regarding whether boards today are receiving and utilizing adequate information and support to address their oversight responsibilities. Far too frequently it seems there is a news report about a breakdown in organization ethics and controls, as well as performance failures across a wide range of industries and organization types.

Events at Volkswagen and the public blowup at a well-known and seemingly successful new economy company, Uber,[21] leading to the resignation of its co-founder and CEO, are two more recent examples. The total fallout and remedies for such performance and governance disruptions can be expensive and lengthy.

Upon reading about each new incident, one has to ask, how could the directors in these organizations not have been aware of serious problems? Did something go wrong in communications and information flows that let this happen?

It seems evident there must have been serious gaps in information supplied to the board, or possibly in the board's understanding and reactions to such information.

A lack of information supplied to boards calls into question whether boards are able to serve as an effective check and balance in the governance of public corporations as well as other organizations. This ability to cross over into an effective checks and balance becomes a concern of the corporate governance lawyer who is not attempting to expand the reach of their authority but has a responsibility for insuring the operability of these checks and balances.

Over the years, courts and eminent legal authorities have set out repeatedly and defined the significant responsibilities of boards for the governance and oversight of the management of public companies. To restate the words of former Delaware Supreme Court Chief Justice E. Norman Veasey, stockholders should

---

[21] Class action litigation was filed in 2022 against Uber. *See* Bos. Ret. Sys. v. Uber Techs. Inc., N.D. Cal., No. 19-cv-06361, 7/26/22.

have the right to expect that "the board of directors will actually direct and monitor the management of the company, including strategic business and fundamental structural changes."

As mentioned earlier, Delaware Supreme Court Chancellor William B. Chandler noted the significant governance and oversight role of the board in his widely publicized opinion in the Disney Corporation Shareholder Derivative suit concerning the hiring, compensation, and firing of Michael Ovitz. Chandler stated, "Delaware law is clear that the business and affairs of a corporation are managed by or under the direction of its board of directors. The business judgment rule serves to protect and promote the role of the board as the ultimate manager of the corporation."

The "ultimate manager of the corporation"—those are very strong words. Some might debate the terminology, preferring instead a phrase like "the ultimate overseer of the corporation." But whether one uses "ultimate manager" or "ultimate overseer" as a designation, a board of directors clearly has significant responsibilities for the welfare of the corporation and its stakeholders.

Serving as an ultimate manager or ultimate overseer requires appropriate information flows to support that role. While there are different types of information flows, this chapter focuses on financial information supplied to boards of directors. We will also discuss two types of information gaps—quantity and quality—that can make it difficult for board members to execute their entire set of responsibilities.

Concurrent with board responsibilities is the lawyer, a part of the checks and balances, aiding in ensuring the board responsibilities are being addressed. An example makes the point: a senior executive (Ph.D. biologist) recounted that in nearly fifty years as a technical manager and director in the food industry he had never interacted with a board of directors over product safety. At the same time, he had interacted with them frequently concerning costs and benefits of product processing innovation/inventions.

This example and our earlier discussion of Boeing and Blue Bell point to the value of the governance lawyer aiding in ensuring these responsibilities are being addressed.

B. Quantity of Information—How Much is the Right Amount? Who Decides?

Regarding quantity of information, we must ask these questions: how *much* information is needed for a body with oversight and increasingly recognized governance responsibilities to perform its functions, especially for a board or a board committee with a critical role in ensuring the welfare of the corporation and the interests of its shareholders? How much information is it realistic to expect a part-time body composed mostly of people from a range of industries, institutions, and professions, which typically meets four to six times a year, to absorb and act upon?

Who decides what data elements will be in the directors' regular information package supplied for the board's periodic meetings? And who decides when special circumstances warrant additional information, and what that information should be? How involved are board members in determining and specifying how much information they will receive for various purposes, when, and in what form?

Typically, when a company is established, the founders and sponsors will work with the initial senior management to lay out a proposed structure for its board, including the board committees that will exist therein and the charters for those committees. The company's management will develop and offer up what they believe to be an appropriate information package for periodic board meetings. Then as time progresses, board members and board committees ask for whatever information they need to achieve effective oversight.

Subsequent issues that may arise include situations where directors may have different views on the amount of information they should receive, creating a need for agenda management, customized information support, or other measures. And sudden, changing circumstances, special events, and unexpected conditions may create a change in the quantity of information needed—as in the case of an unexpected (and possibly unwelcome) tender offer for the company's stock, or when an unexpected organization crisis occurs.

A sizeable amount of routine and ongoing financial information to be supplied to boards may be mandated by organization guidelines, an example being regulators of public companies such as the Securities and Exchange Commission and the stock exchanges. Beyond these mandates, the issue of optimum quantity and design of board information is determined by each organization. In answering the question, board committees often utilize the services of their governance lawyer, outside counsel, and other advisors to identify the information that they should be requesting to support their governance and oversight obligations. They may also use their lawyer and external service providers to assist in performing assessments of internal board processes on a periodic basis.

C. Quality of Information Supplied to the Board—Issues in Measuring Financial Performance

The next question is, what kind of information is needed? Regarding quality of information, consider the nature of the information being supplied, what matters are covered, and how understandable the information is. Also, the timeliness of information is important. On the one hand, board members want to receive information in advance of a meeting to review and absorb it properly. On the other hand, sometimes last-minute developments can affect information previously provided, and there will be a need to ensure that directors receive up-to-date information. While the governance lawyer often ensures the distribution of information, consideration should be given to the lawyer reviewing the adequacy of the information being provided.

Common components of board information include information about an organization's market and business strategy, risk management, measures of financial and operational performance, control structures, management processes, and human resources issues. All of these components of information are important, yet we see the product safety issues of Boeing, of Blue Bell and those discussed earlier. Providing the right kind of financial and related information is an essential part of overseeing a company's performance and prospects.

The design and use of financial and operational measures can be complex for a publicly held company. An obvious requirement for financial information to be supplied to the board is the company's external financial statements and disclosures reported to investors, which securities regulators mandate for board review. These financial statements and disclosures are prepared in accordance with generally accepted accounting principles (GAAP) and supplemented by additional information required by regulators. The information mandated by GAAP and regulators is both voluminous and complex.

GAAP financial statements are widely used, important, and necessary, but they are *not sufficient* to oversee and manage a specific business effectively.

GAAP financial statements are the end product of elaborate and lengthy national and international standards-setting processes designed to achieve consensus among professional accountants, investors, and other stakeholders on how best to portray the value and performance of reporting entities across companies and industries. The resulting body of knowledge utilizes a broad spectrum of concepts, principles, and rules.

GAAP accounting standards represent the eminent thinking and careful deliberation of many experts. The standards are important for broad cross-company use, because they provide a uniform benchmark for external comparisons by investors. Despite the rigor underlying their preparation, GAAP financial statements are inadequate for understanding and running a business at a particular point in time, because they are static and often, complex, and inflexible.

Similarly, every type of organization faces challenges. Economic theory tells us that the division of labor is specific to an organization at a given point in time. Similarly, organization governance structures and processes, and operational needs and priorities, are specific to a firm at a given point. The oversight responsibilities of boards of directors constitute an important check and balance in an organization's ongoing governance structure and operational control system, and such a control system for public corporations must consider more than GAAP financial statements. Boards require relevant information to addressing their oversight responsibilities, as well as information that is clear and understandable.

Boards regularly receive management-provided information. In the case of corporations, if this information takes the form of GAAP financial data, it is likely that they are not getting the full business picture. To oversee, understand, and run a business effectively, one needs to look at corporate performance measures in addition to GAAP. This need has led to custom-tailored internal financial reporting measures used by management and directors of an enterprise. Such internal reporting can be a flexible system, portraying not only standard recurring measures used by management but also selected aspects of operations of particular importance at one time or another. Internal reporting can make certain adjustments to results to consider unit-controllable results and thereby provide additional context and insight into the performance of both business units and the total company. Internal unit reporting may focus on actual versus budgeted cash flows more than unit gross profit or accounting net income.

The governance lawyer has a hand in the preparation and submission of many of these documents. It is a short step for the lawyer to gain the necessary understanding of the documents to assist in the checks and balances structure regarding the substance and content of the documents. Non-GAAP measures offer such an example.

D. Non-GAAP Measures in External Reporting

Because adjusted non-GAAP results can be illuminating and useful to management and directors, some measures may be reported externally to the public and investors, as well as within the business. However, non-GAAP measures used in external reporting have at times been challenged by regulators as misleading to investors. They are deemed misleading on the basis that these measures portrayed only good news and/or were obscuring less favorable performance. The U.S. Securities and Exchange Commission provides substantial guidance on the proper use of non-GAAP measures in external reporting. The guidance also describes SEC enforcement actions for misuse. Internationally, the International Organization of Securities Commissions is a worldwide body of securities regulators in both developed and emerging markets. It has issued pronouncements about non-GAAP reporting as well. Searching these organizations' websites, www.sec.gov and www.iosco.org, for non-GAAP, results in many documents that provide guidance about what is and is not considered acceptable for public reporting of such measures.

In this chapter, we will not attempt to cover the subject on non-GAAP further beyond making these two statements: (1) non-GAAP measures have a useful and legitimate place in reporting about a business, both internally and externally, but care must be taken so they do not mislead investors and other users. (2) An organization's board of directors would be well-advised to understand how an organization's non-GAAP measures are developed and used, and why they are viewed as meaningful in assessing corporate performance, often with the assistance of governance counsel. It is advisable for a board to understand any corporate use of measures that have been challenged by regulators, such as free cash flow or net income excluding the effect of one-time charges, when used in external reporting to investors. The latter has at times been challenged because the label one-time is debatable if such charges have occurred repeatedly, as is sometimes the case with restructuring charges.

Similar consideration must be given to organizations where, due to customs and practice or regulations, certain basic reporting is required. Almost without exception, this basic reporting must be supplemented by the information necessary to govern, oversight and, if required, manage the business, again with the assistance of governance counsel.

E. Using Internal Reporting Design and Cash Flow Monitoring to Understand and Manage Effectively

Ideally, an organization's internal reporting should identify and illuminate the relevant elements of financial and operational performance that are important to the company's success. A good design for internal reporting can also be used to encourage the behaviors and actions that contribute to company success. However, there is an important caveat to be observed when using internal reporting for performance incentive purposes: a design for internal reporting and incentives that doesn't consider existing risks and controls that need to be present can have disastrous consequences. Here again is a role for governance counsel.

The design of a company's internal reporting system to managers and directors is inherently unique to each company. Guidance can be gleaned from benchmarking and understanding the approaches used in peer companies and others and from business publications, but ultimately each company must find its own best design to assess and understand performance. And a best design often needs revision over time, considering changing needs and circumstances.

F. Cash Flow Monitoring—A Key Measure of Performance

An important part of performance measurement that doesn't always receive enough attention in internal reporting to a company's board of directors is *cash flow monitoring*. Cash flows are the lifeblood of a business. There is a reason we hear the phrase "cash is king" often.

Understanding how to interpret cash flows and monitoring cash closely is essential for overseeing and managing a business. Whether a business is a large, multinational, mega-billion-dollar corporation, a mid-size public or private company or partnership, or a small owner and founder-run enterprise, failure to track and manage cash flows effectively can disrupt or even bankrupt a company. Cash flows can be measured effectively in a timely manner. Often, a comparison of budgeted to actual receipts and disbursements can give a clearer financial picture than reported revenues and expenses and net income on, for example, a GAAP income statement. Discussions on the causes of cash flow variances can uncover problems and opportunities without need for approximations or adjustments. The cash flows either did or did not occur within the particular time.

Operational and capital cash flows are concrete results not easily subject to manipulation, especially when measured jointly. Thus, they can serve as a safeguard against efforts to manipulate income through revisions in accruals or reclassifications of operating expenses to capital expenditures. They also can avoid misunderstanding of results that include unbudgeted one-time charges or have been adjusted to exclude such charges. Accurate cash flow information can also help to highlight possible weaknesses in controls and negative developments not apparent in income statement measures. For example, a case where a strong corporate emphasis on customer sales growth, combined with a relaxing of the company's product financing and credit-granting controls, may be increasing risk to an unacceptable level.

Company CFOs, treasurers, and controllers should work together to devise appropriate internal processes and teams for budgeting and measuring cash flows and analyzing anomalies—and for explaining cash flow information to the board in an understandable manner. Relevant board committees such as finance, audit, and nominating and governance will have a significant interest in receiving such information in their check-and-balance and governance roles. An internal audit and the external auditor also may provide input to enhance controls and accuracy. The corporate governance lawyer serves as a check and balance on the information being developed and the usage of the information.

Cash flow information can be complex. For example, the statement of cash flows that is presented in GAAP is viewed by some as arcane and difficult to understand. However, through effective internal measurement and reporting, companies can develop effective methods for presenting cash flow data and interpreting it for the board. A more detailed discussion on cash flow monitoring and reporting, including a model for presenting such data, is set out in chapter VI. The reader is referred to an earlier article on this subject by one of the authors—*see* "Cash Flow Monitoring as a Governance Tool" in *THE CORPORATE BOARD*, March/April 2010.

G. Corporate and Director Obligations for Public Reporting and Disclosure

Since the passage of the Sarbanes-Oxley Act and the later Dodd-Frank Act, several obligations were created for public companies reporting to investors, as well as for board of directors' review of this reporting. Extensive documentation of these requirements can be found in regulatory pronouncements and business and professional publications. Less clearly defined are the requirements pertaining to board review of financial information that could influence an investor's decision to buy or sell stock in a company—what is termed "material information" by the SEC and other regulators—as that information arises. For example, what are the obligations of a director who is given material information in board meeting discussions that the company's executives do not want to disclose to the public yet? Consultation with corporate governance counsel may be needed in such situations.

Appropriate and timely reporting to investors is the direct obligation of a public company's management and can be required in other organizations. However, board oversight of this obligation also requires knowledge about what should be done and when. A discussion of this subject is complex. However, directors can request explanations from a company's corporate governance counsel, CFO, and auditors about the matter.

VI. Monitoring Cash Flows: The Board, the CLO, and the CFO

A. Introduction

As mentioned throughout this book, board responsibilities are complex and continue to grow, with directors being held accountable for the governance, oversight, and, if necessary, management of the organization. This evolution of board responsibilities is long-term and has been further intensified by the pandemic and the economic uncertainty facing organizations of all types today. The chief legal officer (CLO), the chief financial officer (CFO), and other senior officers join the chief executive officer (CEO) as those with the senior-most responsibilities from the management side in ensuring that proper governance, oversight, and management are occurring.

The recent, ongoing developments regarding the survival of certain banks, and perhaps even the future shape of the banking industry, stand as a testament to the fact that the CEO, CFO, and the general counsel (GC) and CLO must join with the board and others in focusing on operational and capital cash flows. Both the CEO and CFO were named as defendants in securities litigation arising from the failures of Silicon Valley Bank and Signature Bank. Too often, companies believed to be healthy have not focused on cash flows, which are often the critical indicator of a company's ability to survive. Troubled companies understand the importance of the cash flows—for some, unfortunately, only when it is too late. The corporate governance lawyer can, as a check and balance, assist in insuring a proper focus on cash flows.

Warren Buffet set out a powerful statement regarding board responsibilities at the 2023 annual meeting of Berkshire Hathaway. He went beyond blaming the chief executives of recently failed banks to blaming the boards of directors for failing to hold the executives accountable. These failures constitute governance and oversight breakdowns. Again, the corporate governance lawyer can assist in monitoring board performance.

B. Case Study

Sophisticated businesses, no matter the size, recognize the importance of tracking cash flows. One of the authors of this book served as the CFO of a diversified holding company that was the managing general partner of two large general partnerships. In each one, the other two general partners were major insurance companies. However, these experiences in partnership settings detailed following are equally applicable to a corporate structure.

Each partnership met quarterly. An important component of these meetings was the CFO's review and discussion of financial and operational results. All of these discussions focused on partnership cash flows—basically, the receipts and disbursements from the normal course of operations, investment income, capital expenditures, and other significant cash items. Cash was addressed comprehensively.

All of the partners agreed that addressing cash flow was more useful than reviewing the income statement because it avoided esoteric accounting entries, as well as footnotes that may be confusing and distracting. The cash data was more understandable and gave a clearer picture of financial performance, a picture that was supported by money in the bank or other liquid assets.

These meetings were an exercise in highly effective governance. The general partner representatives were informed and involved, and their institution had skin in the game. They understood the business and recognized that the tracking of the cash flows was the most effective way to stay on top of the business. They designated the responsibility for reviewing the accounting work of the managing general partner's accounting staff and that of the partnership's external auditor to their respective internal audit staff.

C. Cash Flow Emphasis: Can't Be Overrated

Directors of any company, in any line of business, with the assistance of corporate governance counsel and the CFO would do well to adopt effective techniques to improve their financial oversight. Continuous oversight and interpretation of cash flows by board and senior management are essential. Simply put, cash flows are the organization's lifeblood.

Cash flows can be measured in an effective, timely manner. To reiterate, cash data can be more easily understood and give a clearer financial picture than an income statement. Often, the comparison of budgeted to actual receipts and disbursements gives a much clearer financial picture than reported revenues and expenses and net income on a generally accepted accounting principles (GAAP) income statement. Discussions about the causes of cash flow variances can uncover problems and opportunities without the need for approximations or adjustments. The cash flows either did, or did not, occur within the time.

Operational and capital cash flows are concrete results, not easily manipulated. Therefore, they serve as a safeguard against efforts to manipulate income through revisions in accruals or reclassifications of operating expenses to capital expenditures. Also, they can avoid misunderstanding of results that include unbudgeted, one-time charges, or results that have been adjusted to exclude such charges.

Accurate cash flow information can highlight possible weaknesses in controls and negative developments that are not apparent in income statement measures. For example, in a case where a strong, corporate emphasis on customer sales growth, combined with a relaxing of the company's product financing and credit granting controls, may be increasing risk to an unacceptable level.

As mentioned earlier, certain cash flow information can be complex. For example, the statement of cash flows that is presented in GAAP. This cash flow information is viewed by some as arcane and difficult to understand. Furthermore, it does not provide useful insights of business unit receipts and disbursements.

D. Authority for Cash Flow Management and Cash Control

Who should be given the authority for budgeting the operational cash flows, tracking the actual cash flows, developing the variance reports, and providing explanations of the variances that occur? There are many options. However, an effective approach involves having the company's operating units work with a centralized financial unit such as treasury, financial analysis, or accounting or some combination of these financial units. Typically, the board looks to the CFO to play a major role in structuring the team responsible for budgeting, measuring, and explaining cash flows. Both the internal auditor and the external auditor can provide input to the team and assist in ensuring accuracy. The corporate governance lawyer should be an important element of the associated checks and balances put in place.

E. Analytical Model

An analytical model, as shown in Figure 4, aids in understanding and monitoring operational and capital cash flows. To analyze performance, a model is developed and monitored for each business unit that generates cash flows. The model identifies basic requirements such as working capital, capital expenditures, and debt service and determines if cash flows will be adequate.

If operational cash flows do not provide enough for adequate working capital, do not fund budgeted capital expenditures, or do not cover the required debt service, the business operation is in the crisis zone. The options for the business operation are to fix or to liquidate.

The model also determines a risk-adjusted return on equity. When added to the basic capital requirements, this establishes the market capital requirements. As seen in the cash flows model, if the operational cash flows exceed the basic capital requirements but fall short of market capital requirements, the business

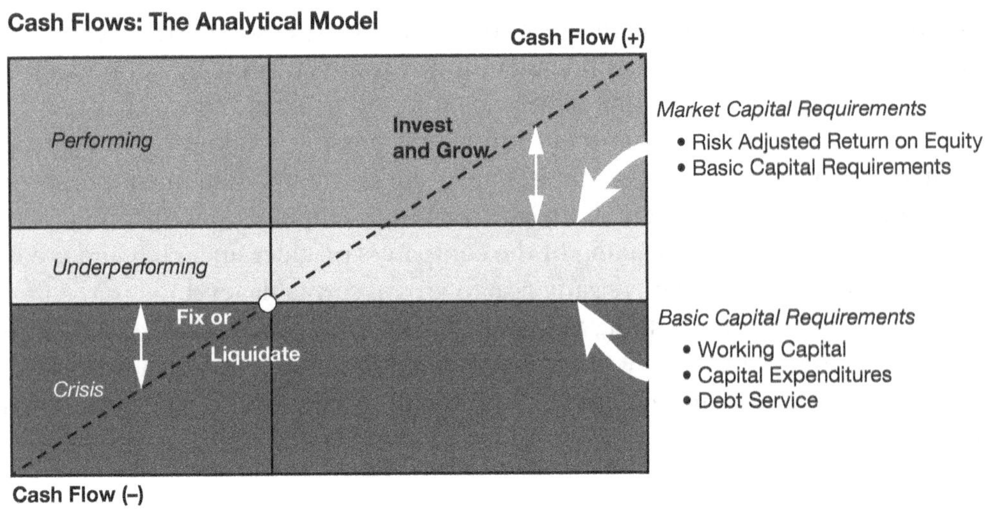

Figure 4

operation is underperforming. It may not be in crisis mode, but steps need to be taken to improve performance.

If the operational cash flows exceed the market capital requirements, the operation is in the performing zone. This shows an opportunity to invest and grow, pay down debt, buy back stock, or make cash distributions to equity holders.

This simple presentation of cash flow data can give the board a clear understanding of whether its firm generates a positive cash flow and if its cash flow is adequate to meet present and future needs. This ability to monitor whether a firm is generating a sufficient cash flow will improve a board's oversight and control system. A board that understands the components of basic capital and market capital requirements, and how they are affected by cash flows, has considerable insight into the risks confronting the firm and can effectively address its oversight responsibilities. Likewise, these basic models are useful to the corporate governance attorney's oversight.

F. Cash Control Activity

Cash control activity comprises two parts. The first involves managing the firm's receipts and disbursements. The second involves monitoring the company-wide cash position.

Controlling a firm's cash inflows and outflows involves monitoring information and control reports between the firm's operations centers and its cash management center; then, the flow of control reports from the cash management center to senior financial management. To effectively monitor cash flows, the firm focuses on the following:

- the varying liquidity requirements and forecasting difficulties facing the different operations centers,

- development and implementation of effective reporting guidelines, and
- the manner and frequency with which periodic variance reports are developed and transmitted.

G. Liquidity Requirements and Forecasting Difficulties

Any attempt at developing an effective cash control system must start with the varying liquidity requirements and forecasting difficulties of the firm. Often, different sectors of a firm have different liquidity needs and face unique problems in developing their forecasts.

Good cash forecasts are built on the correct recognition of the amounts of inflows and outflows expected to take place and when these are expected to occur. The various areas within the firm may be able to forecast the timing for these cash flows, but they may have trouble estimating the amounts involved.

Electricity and gas utilities are examples of firms with this type of problem. As winter and summer approach, forecasters must predict the weather conditions to determine the projected revenues and expenses in the forecasting period. The timing of the revenues does not pose a problem for these firms because most utilities bill their customers in a predetermined balanced manner throughout the month.

With flows for previous forecasting periods available, it is not difficult to accurately estimate the percentage of revenues expected at a point in time. The problem is estimating the total amount of revenue for the period. Similarly, the timing of major outflows is predictable, but the problem is forecasting the amounts (like revenue) that actual weather conditions will affect.

Senior financial management must consolidate cash forecasts early enough to permit them to react to the problems forecasted. It's crucial that the cash management center receives relevant data from different areas within the firm responsible for forecasting so the data can be consolidated in a timely manner. The different areas may require varying lead times, particularly those subject to volatile revenues based on uncontrollable factors such as weather, and those with foreign exchange exposure. As an element of the related checks and balances, the lawyer can observe whether the required steps are being taken.

The timing of the cash forecasts depends on when the various areas can prepare their estimates and, on the time required to consolidate them and prepare the other cash-related data. Once the reporting times are set, they must be observed. This is critical in the early stages of implementing a cash control system.

Each area of activity within the firm is confronted with constant operating pressures, making it difficult for the various areas to complete their forecasts on time. However, those responsible for forecasts need to know that they're being used and are important to the well-being of the entire company. Also, the cash management center needs to respond immediately when the forecasts are not received on time. Those areas that report forecasts late must be contacted as soon as the deadline has been missed, with a follow-up in writing. Another method for enforcing the guidelines is to maintain a checklist of the times when the forecasts are received and forward the checklist to senior financial management.

H. Company-wide Cash Flow Reporting Structures

Similar consideration must be given to shaping the guidelines for reporting the actual cash inflows and outflows. Guidelines must be realistic and recognize the constraints that each of the areas faces.

An important point in the reporting of the inflows and outflows is the tie between cash management and cash control. The same information required for the cash management center can also be used for cash control purposes. A basic structure is set out here (Figure 5).

Controlling the company-wide cash position requires the monitoring of all headquarters, division, and subsidiary bank accounts. Monitoring the headquarters-controlled cash position should be straightforward because the cash management center is in constant communication with the headquarters' accounting staff. Guidelines for maintaining the cashbook on each bank account,

Reporting Relationships for Cash Flows

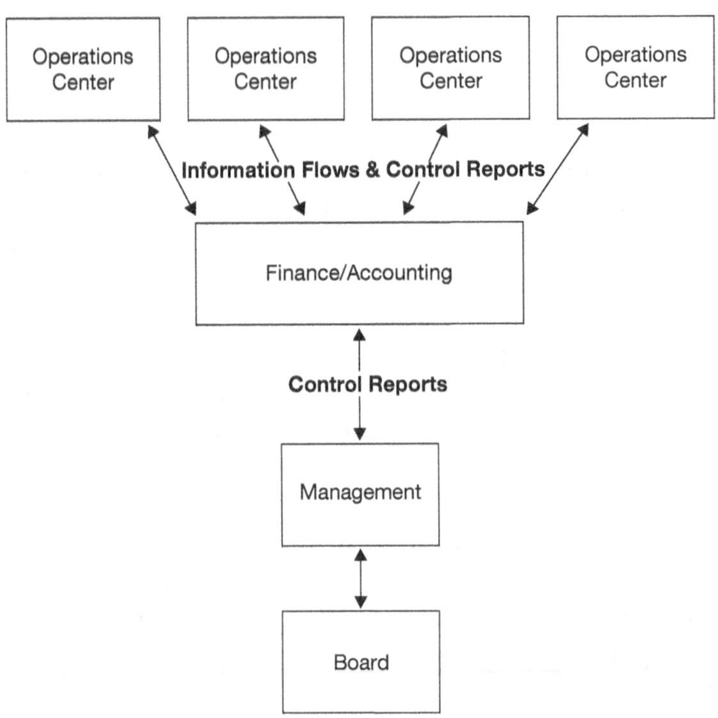

Figure 5

handling the support data, and reconciling the accounts are established in accordance with the internal control requisites.

A way to monitor non-headquarters-controlled accounts on a current basis must be developed. A weekly report indicating beginning and ending balances and total inflows and outflows along with monthly bank reconciliations permits timely monitoring of these accounts.

The importance of a firm's cash flows has focused increased attention on the need for cash control systems. An effective cash control system enables the monthly, weekly, or daily monitoring of operation centers' cash flows. This, in turn, creates an awareness of any unwarranted cash flow variances on a timely basis.

I. Cash Is King

Cash is king not only today—it has always been king.

A common story heard in financial circles describes the damage to a major firm whose board reviewed quarterly financial results solely focused on the income statement. The company's board was told that operating income for the quarter was $490 million and was projected to increase to $525 million in the following quarter. According to this data, everything looked rosy, and no further questions were raised. However, the *cash flow* for the following quarter was projected to be a *negative* $475 million, a $1 billion difference. The firm filed for bankruptcy a few months later. Whether apocryphal or not, the point of the story is clear: ignoring cash flows can be dangerous for corporate health and bad for directors who should know better.

Understanding and monitoring cash flows is an important aid to boards in addressing their continually expanding responsibilities to oversee and direct their firms. Monitoring cash flows is an important tool in effective risk management, serves as a powerful check and balance on other forms of financial and operational reporting, and can aid in fraud detection. CFOs need to coordinate the necessary financial and operational resources and take the lead in monitoring cash flows. In doing so, they create effective presentations to keep board members on top of the truest measure of a company's finances—adequate cash flow. Also, CLOs can and should be an important check and balance regarding the existence and effectiveness of the cash flow management and control structure and their boards' understanding and oversight of the structure.

J. Conclusion

Today's board of directors live in a time of growing governance and oversight responsibilities and expectations. There is a greater likelihood of meeting these expectations if board members have a clear understanding of a company and its financial performance, cash flows, and prospects. Gaps in financial information can undermine a board's ability to perform its role as an important check and balance in the governance, oversight, and operation of the company. A well-designed internal reporting system for measuring and reporting financial performance, coupled with vigilant and active board interest, assisted by the corporate governance lawyer, supports board effectiveness in carrying out their multiple responsibilities. Well-designed internal financial reporting processes and cash-flow monitoring are important components of an effective board information system.

VII. The Board, Management, and the Organization's Intellectual Capital

Chapter III discussed the evolution from tone at the top to substantive checks and balances. It also explained that effective governance includes ethics, values, and a corporate culture attractive to prospective and existing employees—the firm's source of intellectual capital. The importance of these issues is further discussed here.

Today there is increasing recognition that a firm's most valuable assets are its intellectual capital. Although difficult to measure, intellectual capital is credited with a significant portion of productivity increases. Also, it is seen as playing a critical role in the continuation of productivity and profitability improvements. However, rather than the simple financial returns traditionally sought by the owners of physical and financial capital and other key components of production, intellectual capital owners have made it clear they seek to maximize their economic well-being via a combination of monetary and non-monetary compensation. (Note again, the distinguishing of economic well-being from financial well-being, which considers only the monetary compensation one receives. As discussed earlier, economic well-being incorporates both monetary and non-monetary compensation, and can be thought of as the overall quality of one's life.)

One component of the non-monetary compensation today's professionals require is management and board organization leadership based on a leadership framework that incorporates an attitude of responsibility, accountability, and service. Effective board and management interaction helps address the requirement that managers of today's professionals possess and demonstrate a sense of responsibility, a willingness to be accountable, and an attitude of service. To understand this requirement that has been imposed on boards and management, we examine the driving force—the personal governance systems of today's intellectual capital and, then, the issues of management and board responsibility, accountability, and service.

A. Examining Personal Governance Systems

We begin with our examination of the personal governance systems of today's intellectual capital because both management, boards and others in leadership roles must understand the operating platform of today's emerging professionals. We revisit the writings of Aristotle, the Tao Te Ching, and others because of their importance to today's intellectual capital. Similarly, we revisit important recent research on the lifestyle choices which have been made in this country over the past 100 years. Both remind us that an individual's economic well-being may be radically different from their financial well-being. Further, those individuals comprising today's stock of intellectual capital believe that doing well and doing good are not mutually exclusive and that a combination of the two is required to maximize their individual economic well-being.

Boards and management must understand the difference between economic well-being and financial well-being and the complementary relationship between doing well and doing good if their organizations are going to be successful. Equally important, and in contrast with the past, management and boards that attempt to operate from a position of entitlement or privilege will not be tolerated. Intellectual capital is highly mobile and will exercise that mobility unless organization leadership is clear in the recognition of its responsibilities, is forthcoming regarding its own accountability, and is effective in communicating an attitude of service.

These writings we reviewed of Aristotle, the Tao, Isaiah, and the others form the platform that is the one from which today's intellectual capital, today's professionals, operate. Cementing the fact that these writings underpin the platform is the work of Robert Fogel, as mentioned, one of the world's leading economic historians.

Fogel's book, *The Fourth Great Awakening: The Future of Egalitarianism in America*, discusses profound long-term trends in individual work habits. The fundamental lesson for boards and management that emerges from Fogel is that individuals seek to maximize their personal utility and personal satisfaction, not necessarily to maximize their financial wealth. As mentioned earlier, economic well-being is not equal in any sense to financial well-being. Fogel showed that this pattern of behavior has been clear from the economic data available for our country for more than 100 years.

The lesson from this data appears to be even more applicable today. Today's professionals are more cognizant of the activities from which their economic well-being springs, and there are many more options and alternatives available which enable them to achieve an increased level of economic well-being, remote work being one that continues to receive attention in the life balance considerations. Fogel's example of the two toolmakers set out earlier is a straightforward example.

An example that clearly demonstrates the desires of busy professionals to add non-monetary compensation to their lives arises from the New York City Chapter of the Financial Executives International (FEI), discussed in chapter I. Our earlier review of this organization, which consists of approximately 10,000 senior financial executives nationally, is revealing. These individuals are well-compensated and have a set of responsibilities that could involve them thirty hours a day, eight days a week. Yet, when the New York City chapter chose to examine whether its members' skills could be utilized to help make the city of New York a better place to live and work, the response of the members was startling. Instead of grudgingly agreeing to participate, these executives jumped on the opportunities to share experiences with the Office of the State Comptroller, the City University of New York system, the City of New York, Hunter College, the U.S. Government C.F.O.'s Council, the United Nations Institute for Training and Research (UNITAR), the Archdiocese of New York School System, and Baruch College. Those executives did not want to run the organizations or take over the development of the plans of these organizations. These executives simply shared experiences useful to the organizations' efforts to achieve their respective plans.

This response of the FEI members set out in chapter I is consistent with Fogel's research. Fogel's work provides powerful insights for boards and management. The workforce of today—the intellectual capital pool—demands a mix of monetary and non-monetary compensation, and demands availability and flexibility to incorporate a range of activities in their lives to maximize their economic well-being.

Another point for boards and management to consider is the fusion between the positions of economists and the positions of the spiritualists and the philosophers. To many, these views often have been seen to be divergent, in the sense that the economics of capitalism is said to drive people toward greed and exploitation via the simple maximization of financial well-being. However, what economists have always said is that *individuals will seek to maximize their economic well-being*. Interestingly, for more than 5,000 years, spiritualists and philosophers have been telling individuals *how to maximize their economic well-being*: recognize the moral law within, recognize and respect the rights of others, and lead a life of service. There is a common message coming from all sides, rather than positions that are diametrically opposed to the other.

B. Management and Boards—Responsibility, Accountability, and Service

After examining the personal governance systems of today's professionals, we turn to the issues of management and board responsibility, accountability, and service. With their training, their astuteness, their awareness of global events, and their requirement for an appropriate mix of monetary and non-monetary compensation, today's professionals understand and are comfortable with the mobility available to themselves. There is no reluctance to call upon this mobility if it is going to permit the achievement of a higher level of economic well-being. As such, today's professionals call for management to have a comprehensive understanding of and a willingness to address their responsibilities. They expect management to be accountable and to put appropriate sets of checks and balances in place for their own activities which will ensure accountability on the part of all the involved parties. Perhaps most importantly, they want management to bring an attitude of service. Simultaneously, there is an increasing level of intolerance toward managers that seek to operate from positions of entitlement and privilege.

Not only is any attitude of management entitlement or privilege out, responsible management is a mandate from today's professionals. Smart and well-trained, they will gravitate to working environments where management is respected. Management has the critical responsibility of understanding where the firm or organization is, and where it wants to be in the future. Management must select the path to be traveled to reach this future destination and the management tools to be used on the journey. All of this must be communicated effectively to their professionals. Monitoring the journey and redetermining the road of travel must be done along with providing day-to-day leadership.

The concern is how many of today's managers and board members understand the factors Fogel sets out as being critical to enabling employees to maximize their personal well-being. Without this understanding, the organization could focus only on monetary compensation and wonder why the productivity of their intellectual capital assets continues to fall below expectations.

The issue of accountability facing boards and management drives right out of the ongoing evolution in organization governance. Organization governance is learning the lesson that history has taught regarding political governance—that monarchies and dictatorships, those seemingly simple, effective governance mechanisms, have consistently failed because they failed to get the tone at the top correct. Organization governance has erred similarly by believing that the route to better governance was simply to improve the tone at the top. What is required is a system of checks and balances, a proper balancing of the elements of organization governance.

As mentioned earlier, in case one wonders why there has been a failure in the tone at the top, and why these checks and balances in our systems of political governance and organization governance are required, we have only to look to Lord Acton's famous quote, "Power corrupts, and absolute power corrupts absolutely." Preceding Acton, there was the Roman poet Ovid, who summed it up so well 2,000 years ago when he spoke of the challenges that face individuals in life, "The better things of life I see and approve, the worse things of life I follow." History has shown us that monarchs and dictators, and many other leaders, have known what needed to be done, but frequently failed to act appropriately.

Those two quotes give a clear message. Democracy, with its seemingly onerous and time-consuming checks and balances, emerged because of the consistent failures of monarchies and dictatorships. Organization governance must institute standards of accountability and implement appropriate checks and balances. Boards and management must ensure that these checks and balances exist at all levels within the organization, beginning with themselves.

The requirement that an attitude of service be demonstrated is not surprising. Remember, the leaders in all walks of life who have been truly revered and remembered are those that brought an attitude of service to their positions. When someone thinks of George Washington, they think of his service to his country. When one thinks of Abraham Lincoln, one remembers the famous line from the Gettysburg Address, "Four score and seven years ago, our fathers brought forth upon this continent, a new nation, conceived in liberty, and dedicated to the proposition that all men are created equal," to recognize Lincoln's attitude of service toward his country grounded in fundamental moral principles. Get past the focus on political issues, and you understand the underlying message of Dr. Martin Luther King, Jr. His message focused on human dignity, creation, redemption, forgiveness, and brotherhood. Finally, we've all read or heard the words of John F. Kennedy, "Ask not what your country can do for you, ask what you can do for your country." Boards and management are not only there to serve the shareholder and the customer, but also to help its employees grow and meet their individual goals. Again, an attitude of privilege and entitlement on the part of boards and management will not be tolerated.

In closing, we have two thoughts. First, having been students of and participants in a broad range of management structures over the years, it has become more and more evident that management is not a zero-sum game. Management is either a win-win or a lose-lose situation. It is not about taking from one and giving to another. It is about creating a structure that optimizes for all involved. A firm can focus simultaneously on maximizing returns to its shareholders and being a good citizen.

An example is provided by the controller of one of the largest companies in the world who told this story about her team of employees participating in one of the Financial Executives International (FEI) projects we discussed earlier. At the completion of their project, the Controller's team asked to speak to her. The team of senior executives, said, "There are three points we want to mention: First, we were complimented to be picked to be on the team; second, we were proud to be able to discuss our firm's work in this area; and, third, we learned a tremendous amount from the interaction with the other firms and the Office of the State Comptroller." This was a simultaneous maximization—a win-win for the Office of the State Comptroller, the firm's employees, and the firm. As Aristotle, the Tao, and the others set out, in giving—in sharing their experiences—the firm and its employees received benefits they did not anticipate. Organization leadership is not a zero-sum game.

Second and lastly, do not be afraid to be correct morally. You should never presume you possess the mantle to set moral standards for others, but do not fail to observe your own. At the end of the day, you must live with yourself and the moral law within you.

Boards and management currently face, and will continue to face, issues with moral implications. Boards and management, not management alone, will need to address these and, where appropriate and if there is a consensus, set out the organization's viewpoints. Management's and the board's approach to these difficult issues will be observed and either respected or disrespected by the organization's intellectual capital.

VIII. Board Member Selection and Board Interaction

Steering an organization forward to accomplish its mission, please its shareholders, and reach new goals while being on top of governance and mitigating risk is a complex challenge for boards of directors. However, it is a challenge that every organization must be prepared to tackle well. As we have stated earlier, retired Chief Justice Veasey makes clear, "the board of directors will actually direct and monitor the management of the company, including strategic business and fundamental structural changes," and retired Chancellor Chandler further confirmed these responsibilities.

The Federal Reserve made this clear on its website. While bank boards may delegate "the day-to-day routine of conducting the bank's business to its officers and employees, the board cannot delegate its responsibility for the consequences of unsound or imprudent policies and practices." The Fed's settlement with the Wells Fargo board required the Wells board to redevelop and resubmit its plan for governing Wells and its plan for overseeing Wells. The Fed recognized the Wells board's duties to govern and to oversight as two distinct responsibilities and was critical of their initial efforts in developing these plans. As such, board member selection and board member interaction is critical.

A. Board Member Selection—Mission Critical

Board duties of governance, oversight, and management are mandated legally and supported by economic fundamentals. The board of each organization must determine its respective approach to defining, implementing, and continuing to monitor and modify the addressing of the duties. Boards work closely with the corporate governance lawyer and others regarding duties of the organization. Likewise, the board will work closely with the CEO, the CFO, and others depending on the nature of the organization.

Selecting the appropriate board members is challenging and only becoming more challenging. The retired CEO of a major oil and gas firm shared his experience in an audience of senior executives and board members. A state governor contacted him to step in for the CEO of a sizeable natural resources company who had died in an automobile crash. Reluctantly, he accepted. He explained that, on arriving and meeting the board members, he became aware that, while several of them had senior level executive and board experience, none had relevant natural resource industry experience. The deceased CEO was the only one with any depth of experience because there were no other officers on the board.

A distinct contrast with this is the board inherited and further developed by Mike Eisner and Frank Wells at Walt Disney when they were retained—Eisner as CEO and Wells as President in 1983.

The Disney board was loaded with individuals with a deep-seated relationship with and understanding of Disney, who brought insights on issues embedded in the decisions facing Disney. These board meetings were alive with interaction, exchanges, and thorough discussions of the issues and subjects under consideration.

Desired attributes for a board include members who are informed, involved, have skin in the game, understand their responsibilities, are accountable to the ultimate owners (of whom three at Disney were on the board and two of those held senior executive positions), and have an attitude of service. The directors at the outset and those that joined during that period of Eisner and Wells leadership possessed many, if not all, of those attributes.

B. Board Interaction—Equally Critical

Eisner and Wells inherited and further developed this makeup. Keep in mind this 1983–1995 time period was when Disney really blossomed. This was when Disney strengthened its foundation and laid the groundwork to move forward. But moving forward was not assured.

Walt Disney was a complex company at that time, struggling to define itself and clarify plans in multiple directions. It was not a company without problems. About the time Ron W. Miller, the son-in-law of Walt Disney, was named president and CEO in 1983 after thirty years at Disney, Roy E. Disney, the son of Walt's brother (Roy O. Disney) and also a 30-year employee, resigned from the board. Then, two months later, he rejoined the board as the vice chairman, a position he held from 1984 to 2003. Sharon Disney Land also was on the board. These groups of family members controlled between 15 and 20 percent of the Disney stock. Ownership was present and deeply involved.

Former and current Disney senior executives were on the board, along with outside directors with insights and skills important to Disney. Eisner and Wells worked with these individuals and, rather than being intimidated, they drew from this pool of experience and moved Disney forward in a remarkable manner.

In simple terms, Disney's success under Eisner and Wells in the period 1984–1995 was spectacular. If someone invested $10,000 in Disney stock in September 1984, it was worth approximately $160,000 by July 1994. While

$10,000 invested in the S&P Index over this period would have had an approximate value of $56,000.

Eisner and Wells retained talent on the board. When Gary Wilson, EVP and CFO of Walt Disney Productions, became vice chairman of Northwest Airlines, he remained on the Disney board.

When Frank Wells died in a helicopter crash in 1994, the hiring of Michael Ovitz was facilitated by Irwin Russell, an experienced entertainment lawyer and chair of the Disney compensation committee, and Raymond Watson, a long-time (external) director and member of the compensation committee, who was serving as the interim chairman of Disney when Eisner and Wells were hired.

Directors added during this period included, Leo J. O'Donovan, S.J., a Jesuit priest who was president of Georgetown University; Reveta F. Bowers, a highly respected youth educator; and Sidney Poitier, the distinguished actor. All three brought unique Disney-oriented talents to the board. The president of Georgetown contributed to the ongoing discussion of the moral tone of Disney movies, the educator spoke to the state of young people, and the actor had ongoing interactions with the acting community.

The collection of talent and experience on the Disney board could tackle issue after issue. Individuals with significant director experience will sense the depth and breath of the board discussions that occurred. This knowledge base and sense of Disney, and its operations under the leadership of Eisner and Wells, contributed to organization governance of unique quality.

Disney's success during this period was driven, at least in part, by a deeply experienced board. The board understood Disney and its many operations, with substantial ownership activity involved, working with a leadership team comfortable with an open interchange among the directors and other involved resources. These directors underscored the issues of governance, oversight, and management Disney was addressing. They were informed, involved, had skin in the game, they understood their responsibilities, were accountable in addressing them, and brought an attitude of service to their roles.

The contrast between the board of Disney during this period and the board the retired CEO at the natural resources company inherited when he succeeded the deceased CEO speaks for itself. Assembling a board with the talent of that Disney board is a challenge, but failing to do so appears to be less and less of an option.

The ongoing issues discussed here regarding Wells Fargo and Boeing and their boards are a further confirmation. Current and future litigation involving each of the firms may well follow those directors to their graves and beyond.

It will not be surprising to see more and more attention paid to the directly applicable experience of directors and their independence from the CEO. The settlement requirement that airplane safety experience be added to the Boeing board, Blue Bell's absence of a safety committee, and the comments mentioned from the Ph.D. biologist, all call for properly experienced directors.

Whether the board is entirely comprised of one-eyed martians is irrelevant. Whether they have directly applicable experience, and whether they are sufficiently independent of the CEO may, in most situations, be the critical factors.

IX. CONCLUSION

A. Current Issues

As we have discussed earlier in this volume, there is an ongoing controversy over ESG issues. To refresh, ESG refers to environmental, social and governance issues. The least controversial of these issues is corporate governance, which is at the heart of the judicial decisions and business issues we have discussed throughout this volume. The more controversial areas, however, are environment, particularly regarding climate change matters, and social, usually involving diversity and related matters. ESG Issues have become highly politicized and controversial in the business community, and this has manifested itself in legislation at the state level and in shareholder litigation. It is beyond the scope of this book to address these issues in any great depth. However, it should be noted that many states have adopted anti-ESG legislation that purport to limit the ability of those states, particularly with respect to their public employee retirement plans, to do business with entities that boycott industries based on ESG criteria.

Similar issues arise with respect to Diversity, Equity, and Inclusion (DEI) initiatives, particularly in light of the landmark Supreme Court decision striking down so-called affirmative action programs. *See, Students for Fair Admissions Inc. v. President* & *Fellows of Harvard College*, 600 U.S. 181 (2023). Again, this is beyond the scope of what we intend to address in this book, but we do note its potential effect on organizational governance issues. We do, however, refer the reader to chapter VII in this book where we discuss the interaction between an organization's intellectual capital, the board and executive management.

Much of the ESG litigation has been brought by shareholders against companies allegedly overtouting their ESG accomplishments, as opposed to companies that are doing little with regard to ESG. One suit filed in June 2023 against American Airlines, its employee benefit's committee and others alleged that the defendants "breached their fiduciary duties in violation of ERISA by investing millions of dollars of American Airlines employees' retirement savings with investment managers and investment funds that pursue leftist political agendas through ESG strategies, proxy voting, and shareholder activism—activities which fail to satisfy these fiduciaries' statutory duties to maximize financial benefits in the sole interest of the plan participants. Another suit involving another major U.S. airline, is typical of what have become known as "greenwashing" suits.

That suit alleges that the airline's claims of carbon neutrality are false and misleading. Unfortunately, on many levels ESG has become a hot button political issue applied broadly by both supporters and anti-ESG parties with little understanding of the core issues.

B. The Ongoing Evolution of Governance Responsibilities

Governance is a fluid area, both in terms of legal guidance and business analysis. As we have discussed herein, *Caremark* duties were first enunciated in the late 1990s with the advisory that these should be difficult hurdles for plaintiffs to overcome.

Fast forward about twenty-five years, when *Marchand* and *Boeing* suggest that those hurdles may not be so steep after all. Although many of the principles of sound governance are somewhat eternal dating back to Aristotle and the Prophet Isaiah, times change, and governance must adapt to the changing times. That is why we have new focus on mission critical areas that can vary from one business to another.

It behooves boards, management, and the corporate governance lawyer to keep abreast of these developments and to implement solutions wisely and effectively.

APPENDIX I

"The CFO and Public Policy,"

H. Stephen Grace, Jr. Ph.D.

The Corporate Report—Second Quarter 1997

THE *CORPORATE* REPORT

EDITION NO. 21 A FORUM FOR SENIOR EXECUTIVES 2ND QUARTER 1997

Michael Adams, President, Environics Research Group, Toronto
Sex in the Snow: How well do you know who you're talking to? 6

Francoise Bertrand, Chairperson, Canadian Radio-television and Telecommunications Commission, Hull, Quebec
The Empowerment of Women in the Workplace 13

Rowland W. Fleming, President & CEO, The Toronto Stock Exchange, Toronto
The TSE After Bre-X 17

Stephen Grace, President, H. S. Grace & Company, Houston
The CFO and Public Policy 25

Thomas Kierans, President & CEO, C. D. Howe Institute, Toronto
The Nuts and Boas of Federalism 37

Huguette Labelle, President, Canadian International Development Agency, Hull, Quebec
International Development: Everybody's Business 49

Roger Landry, President & Publisher, *La Presse*, Montreal
The Media and the Unity Issue 55

Dana Mead, Chairman & CEO, Tenneco, Houston
Going Global • Success on the Front Line 61

Brian Mulroney, former Prime Minister of Canada, Montreal.
Canada in the 21st Century 67

Rob Rae, former Premier of Ontario, Toronto
Montreal's Fate and Ours 75

James Stanford, President and CEO, Petro-Canada, Calgary
Globalization and the Petroleum Industry in :Canada 79

Thomas Volpe, Senior Vice-President 8c CFO, The Interpublic Group of Companies, New York
Globalization the Right Way: Managing the Financial Process. 88

L. R. Wilson, Chairman & CEO, BCE Inc., Montreal
Telepresence: The Challenge and the Opportunity of the Future 94

 Subscriptions are C5245.00 a year (four editions—please use the form on page 104). Reports are mailed first class at Montreal. Please send all submissions for publication, subscription orders and changes of address to: *The Corporate Report,* 982 Egan Avenue, Verdun QC Canada H4H 1 W7. Telephone: (514) 769-1184 Fax: (514) 769-1185 Email: edi500@netcom ca

PRINTED IN CANADA BY DATA RESOLUTIONS

THE CFO AND PUBLIC POLICY

H. Stephen Grace, Jr., Ph.D.
President, H. S. Grace & Company

Address to the Forbes Chief Financial Officers Forum, Rio Mar, Puerto Rico, February 10, 1997

Today I am putting before you a very simple message, and that is that we, as senior financial executives, can contribute significantly to the resolution of today's fiscal, social, and public policy problems. We can do it in a manner that utilizes our strongest skill sets and we can do it in a manner that benefits not only ourselves but our employees and our organizations.

Now that's a broad, sweeping statement to make. Each of us could be saying to ourselves, how in the world could we do that? How do we contribute with all of the things—work pressures, time constraints—that we face? Well, as we look today at the work of a group of over 50 senior financial executives, a group of our peers, what we'll see is not only the significance of their work for the recipient organizations, but we will also see clearly the powerful impact that this work has had on these individuals, their fellow employees and their organizations. So there are two areas of focus: first, we will look at the contributions that were made and how we used our strongest skill sets-our financial management skills, in making these contributions; and second, we will to look at the depth and breath of the benefits that flowed back from these activities.

In 1993, the New York Chapter of the Financial Executives Institute established a small, informal committee to investigate what would represent a totally new area of activity for the chapter. The mission of the committee was quite simple, and that was to determine how we could use our financial management skills to help make New York City a better place in which to live and work. The committee consisted of Frank Borelli, chief financial officer of Marsh & McLennan, Mike Esposito, then chief administrative officer of Chase, Tom Jones, executive vice-president of Citicorp, Bob Roath, then controller and now CFO at RJR Nabisco, and myself. We set about looking at the types of assistance we might offer, those organizations to whom we might reach out and, very importantly, what would be the attitudes of our members toward undertaking this type of activity.

One of the first tasks we undertook was to create project guidelines. The guidelines defined where we were, what we had to offer and how we were going to offer it. They represented a very important first step. Each project would be well defined and directly applicable to our skill sets. The projects would be brought to closure within relatively short time frames—a very important requirement. We were not going to enter into undefined, open-ended commitments to organizations—that was not what we saw as our role relative to what we felt we were able to deliver.

Also, projects would be jointly determined. And, the projects would offer assistance in the achievement of missions or goals, not in defining missions and goals, nor in evaluating performance. We weren't coming in putting a gun to someone's head about how they or their fellow organization members were or were not achieving their respective missions. We certainly felt that the defining of missions and goals and the evaluation of performance were important issues, but our belief was that, if individuals wanted to undertake those activities, they should do this on an individual basis by becoming involved in an organization, learning how it operated, and then participating in that type of definitional and guiding work. We, as an organization, were simply looking to use our financial management skills to assist these organizations in the achievement of their missions and goals.

Regarding the last couple of guidelines—no financial assistance—we were all already called upon for every dollar we and our organizations could give. That's not where we were coming from. And we were not going to compete with nor replace consulting firms. They have a role and an important role. Again, we were simply going to utilize our skills.

As we turned to identifying those organizations whom we might assist, very quickly the scope of the organizations broadened from simply government-related entities to include non-profit and, importantly, certain programs of religious institutions which we felt benefited the City of New York and the environment in which we lived and worked. Faith Whittlesey, former ambassador to Switzerland and currently president of the American Swiss Foundation, pointed us toward the Archdiocese of New York's School System. Faith is not a Catholic but, in effect, said, "Those people make a critical contribution to New York by educating a wide range of students and, even more importantly, in many areas of the city they are the only source of continuity and stability out there."

Interestingly, as we broadened our scope of activities from its initial focus—government entities—as we moved into the non-profits, and even into certain programs of religious institutions, our board's approval was unanimous. Their feeling was that we needed to expand from solely government entities; we needed to move into the non-profits. The board was right saying that's where we needed to go and put our financial and business experience to work.

At this point, without being patronizing to my good friend Tom Volpe, the project actually entered into what I call the "Volpe Era." Tom had been strongly involved from the start in this initiative and, even before he took over as chapter president, was driving this activity forward, looking at the organizations to whom we needed to reach out. It was Tom who created the relationship with Carl McCall, the state comptroller. He also created the relationship with David Caputo, the president of Hunter College. We'll talk later about the projects we did with both of these entities. Tom has never ceased looking for and finding organizations we could assist with our skills.

At the same time we were establishing relationships with several organizations, we were passing on other organizations that had been brought up for consideration. In many cases, these were outstanding organizations which had a great deal to offer the city, but there simply wasn't a fit between our skill sets and their needs. We, as a group, did not have something to offer them in terms of our financial skills; however, many of these organizations were recommended to our members—that they consider participating in these organizations on an individual basis. Again, throughout this process, we were continuing to attempt to read where our members were with regard to these activities and, very early, member feedback began to surface. And there was continued strong support from the chapter presidents—I'll come back to this.

Let's take a moment now and examine some of the projects undertaken—what we did in connection with these projects—in order to demonstrate the nature of the contributions that were being made. Carl McCall, comptroller of the State of New York, and his first deputy Comer Coppie, an outstanding individual in his own right, and the other deputies (a great group to work with) basically said to us, "Look, we've got some challenging issues with regard to our payroll system. It was originally developed in 1970, it's outdated, with everybody saying it's on the verge of collapse. However, we're talking about a major expenditure, $20 million to $40 million, to put a new system in place. We'd like you to give us some assistance by sharing your experiences with the various aspects of payroll systems." In other words, they were not asking us to build the system, but only to share experiences with them that would assist in visualizing their alternatives and options.

When you think about it, what better group could Carl McCall and Corner Coppie have come to? We are out there living with payroll and human resource issues every day. So what did we do? How did we address this project? Frank Gatti of *The New York Times* put together a team that included The New York Times Company, Marsh & McLennan and The Interpublic Group of Companies, all of whom approached the problem differently—three different approaches to the issues. One firm's systems combined the human resources and payroll elements, the second one kept them completely separate, and the third had created a system that was a hybrid. So, in a full day of meetings, the state comptroller's staff got a detailed briefing from these three companies on what worked and what didn't work in each of their systems—their foresight, their hindsight, the issues they felt they faced going forward and, very importantly, how they built a business case to justify the expenditures they had made for their respective systems.

Interestingly, but not surprisingly, all of those in attendance at the meeting felt that a great deal had been accomplished. A great deal had been learned not only by the comptroller's staff but by all of those in attendance. Equally interesting was the fact that, subsequently, the legislature appropriated $5 million to begin the work of designing and implementing a new payroll system, after having twice turned down requests for funding. Whether or not our discussions contributed to the decision to fund will never be known, nor it is particularly important. What is apparent is that, as a result of the sharing of experiences, the comptroller's staff was able to come back describing completely neutral, objective advice that had been given regarding the issues involved in the design and implementation of a new system and how these issues could be addressed. They were also able to build an effective case for a non-revenue producing expenditure.

Just as interestingly, we can see how this project fit right into the project guidelines we had developed. Here was a well-defined project which required certain preparation, but which was basically completed with one full-day meeting. The project team continues to stand ready to address various issues and questions which arise from the comptroller's staff as they move forward, but basically the project was brought to completion in the sharing of information and expertise.

The second project for the state comptroller was internal control. They, in effect, said, "Our interests are twofold: we want to fully understand the issues associated with internal control and we want to examine how internal control can be marketed in a large-scale organization." They went on to say they wanted to do it not only for their own operation, but for other government entities in New York State, and to put together a manual that would be available to other government entities both within and outside the state. We assembled a team—people from Philip Morris, Equitable, NYNEX, and my colleagues at Zolfo Cooper—who could offer their experience with a wide range of "troubled companies." Several meetings occurred, spaced over a number of months, with major presentations by the various groups, and today a manual is in the process of being put together. At the start of the initial meeting the comment was made that this may be the first time that senior members of government and private industry have ever sat down together to address this type of issue. There it was happening—a meeting which may have indeed been a first. And it was natural for us to step in and undertake this defined project, within its relatively short-term time frame. We made our contribution, experiences were shared among all of the parties in a series of meetings, and the state comptroller's team was well prepared to move into the preparation of a manual which the total team agreed to review at a later date.

The risk management project for the state comptroller was interesting. The state comptroller came to us and said, "You know, we've got a problem with our firemen and policemen. We self-insure and, of course, those people experience a large number of injuries on the job with permanent disability in a number of cases." They went on in general to say, "We know we can do better and we believe we can benefit here also by sharing experiences and would like to discuss that." We reflected on this matter saying to ourselves, "This seems to be slightly different from what we had in mind." At the same time, it did appear that we could assemble a team, and we did—people from Reliance Insurance, Colgate-Palmolive and Equitable.

What happened in the subsequent meetings among the state comptroller's officers, the firemen state union leaders and our companies, was amazing. We marvelled at it ourselves. Because the state self-insures in many areas, it does not have the benefit of insurance carriers coming to assist them, demonstrating ways to reduce the incidence of injuries and, even more importantly, offering insight when an injury occurs as to how to get the injured person to the right type of care initially, and, subsequently, how to assist him or her throughout the rehabilitation process. To say these disability and rehabilitation issues were of concern to all parties involved is an understatement. The state comptroller's office, and also the state leaders of the firemen's union, jointly made clear the seriousness of the firemen's plight. They pointed out that, while many people may think that a fireman getting disabled and subsequently receiving almost 100% of his salary for the rest of his life would seem to have it made, this was far from the case. Both New York State and the union were well aware of the facts and cited statistics to prove that these individuals have a higher divorce rate, and their psychological state is known to be much worse. The bottom line is these union members were being seriously damaged by the entire situation.

So what we had was both the union and the government jointly looking at ways to address a very serious issue. At the same time, here were our people saying, "Wow! We can help. We know this business. We understand how you get your hands around people when they're hurt, how to get them to the right medical care, and how you work with them through the rehabilitation stages." You could just see it right on the faces of these executives that they could assist in improving the well-being of the firemen. And they were saying, we must do this, we have the ability to contribute and the opportunity is right there in front of us. Clearly a situation where all of the parties were winners. Yet once again, a well-defined, short-term project. It happened in the form of a series of meetings, the assistance was provided, and everyone moved on.

I'll come back to some of the other projects for the state later. Hunter College president David Caputo knew he wanted industry input in the areas of information technology and management practices. In the case of information technology, he wanted an outside assessment of the technology, not only in the classroom, but also with regard to servicing the university as a whole. Our chapter's Information Technology Roundtable took on this project and we'll see in a moment exactly what Caputo had to say about those results. In summary, very positive benefits flowed to the university. The Corporate Advisory Council, a slightly different type of body, requires a longer term of involvement. Our members can step on and off of the council as their other requirements mandate. Here, Caputo was seeking our advice, not only from a curriculum standpoint, but also with regard to the management of the institution. Again, a natural for our group to share views, to provide ideas drawing on our depth in particular areas.

When you look at our work for the Archdiocese of New York School System and simply scan the projects undertaken, you can see their interest in discussing things such as purchasing procedures, cash management procedures, record retention procedures, some pension fund administration details, policies and procedure manuals—all of which were like water off a duck's back to the group of us. We are addressing matters like these literally all of the time. They are subjects with which we live, which we grew up with as we moved through a range of managerial responsibilities, and they are naturals for us to address by putting together small teams, stepping in and making our respective contribution. They are not, however, matters in which the archdiocese has expertise.

The enrolment projection model for the archdiocese represented a slightly different type of project. A very interesting situation—they came to us and, in effect, said, "You know, we're trying to develop a model to project enrolment on the secondary level and we could use some of your experience." So, the controller of one of our companies assigned a team of actuaries. What a natural thing for these actuaries (who build models all the time) to undertake! They stepped in and, before we knew it, the archdiocese was telling us the model had been used in their decision to buy a new facility. Furthermore, the enrolment at that facility had gone up 100% in one year and they are expecting it to increase another 100% the subsequent year. In other words, a fourfold increase in two years. Additionally, the Archdiocese of Chicago had become aware of the model and asked the Archdiocese of New York if they could get clearance for Chicago to use it.

Clearly the work being performed was benefiting the recipient organizations, but what about our people? Just take the enrolment projection model project. The controller was telling me his actuaries were literally "on the moon" after undertaking the development of the model. Here they were, using their strongest skill sets, able to step right in and make a contribution to people who, as the actuaries put it in their own words, have a mission. Whether the actuaries were Catholic or not, they saw people out there educating the youth of New York. And these actuaries saw their ability to assist these people in a very valid, worthwhile mission. And they made it happen!

The relationship has continued. The actuaries call the school periodically and offer assistance with the school's database—natural areas in which their skill sets can be utilized. Nothing defined, nothing required, but a high-quality, ongoing relationship which is reflective of the flow of benefits coming back to our members and their employees.

The second area of focus has to do with the benefits flowing back to us—not only the financial executives, but also our fellow employees and our organizations.

I don't think there's any stronger commentary that can be made about these benefits than our own chapter members' comments. At the start of my remarks, I said we were very concerned about what our members' responses would be toward these activities, because all of them are time constrained, facing tremendous work pressures. We all know and understand that is the world in which we live. What would be their response?

Just look at these comments: "I'm been a member for over 10 years. This is the most important thing the chapter has ever done." When that member made that statement to me, I remember thinking how I feel that we do a lot of important things; yet he thinks this is the most important thing we have ever done. And he was certainly an individual who had been closely involved with leadership of the chapter.

Another member said, "We cannot just have monthly meetings at which we eat and talk, we must do something worthwhile." A third person, a very thoughtful individual involved for many years as a leader of the chapter, said, "I have been participating in board meetings for years at which we discussed membership and programs, now we are addressing important topics." The final comment and a very pertinent remark: "We must do this work." A very senior person at one of the largest companies in the world: "We must do this work." So you say to yourself that our members are seizing upon these activities in a manner that is clearly telling us something.

It's this level of response that surprised us. The biggest surprise we had was the way the group of members seized upon the need to do this work. So you ask yourself, what's driving this depth of commitment, this interest in undertaking the right amount of this work, not casting aside your other responsibilities, but incorporating it along with them? And I think at least part of this drive can be explained by looking at certain writings over the centuries.

You go back to Aristotle, some 2,300 years ago in Book II of *The Politics*. He's arguing against Plato and Socrates, by the way, who said in the perfect state everything should be held in common, nothing should be owned individually. Aristotle gives a number of reasons why he feels this concept will not work. But he says the major reason is because you deprive man of his greatest pleasure, and that is giving of himself. Apply this to our chapter members—what are our people giving? They're giving their two most precious commodities in actuality, because money is probably not one of their most precious. Their most precious gifts are probably their time and their energy, because they already have so many calls on them.

Look at Immanuel Kant. He says the two things that awe him most—and if you've ever read Kant, it's an amazing exercise just to undertake the effort, and here he is not saying he's the greatest thing that ever walked the earth—he says that there are two things that awe him the most—the starry heavens and the moral law within. He says that there is a moral law operating within us.

Pope John XXIII says it slightly differently. He talks about a common effort of free individuals for the good of society and he says, "It is . . .the fruit and expression of a natural human tendency, almost irrepressible in human beings—the tendency to join together to attain objectives which are beyond the capacity and means of single individuals." Very powerful remarks—all three quotes. You look at these and there is a direct linkage to what is going on with our members, to those benefits flowing back.

We'll come to Carl Jung in a few moments. He makes a very important statement about what happens when the moral law is not observed by people. But let's step in another direction for a moment and consider the commentary that has come from the recipient organizations.

State comptroller Carl McCall says, "Our working with the Financial Executives Institute has shown us that business and government are facing similar issues and that when we come to the same table and work through these things together it benefits us. In each of these projects, FEI's input has been a valued part of the decision-making and implementation process and the results show the first steps toward improved efficiency and effectiveness." Right there our role is set out. Our input has been a valued part of the decision-making and implementation process they undertook. We are not there to define their missions or goals but only to assist in the achievement of those missions and goals.

We go next to the comments by monsignor Tom Bergin, vicar of education. "The good sense and practical approaches to our work provided by the members of FEI placed our management of education in a different light. As a result of discussions we were able to redesign approaches, husband resources and result in cost savings." Hunter College president David Caputo, speaking regarding the review of technology undertaken: "The efforts of the Technology Roundtable resulted in critical recommendations being made which have been incorporated in the formulation of a reorganization plan put out to the Hunter College community." And, just one last comment from the superintendent of schools, "School administrators approach things from a different vantage point than businesspeople, but having interested people from business look at our work and suggest approaches has enabled us to plan better."

Notice what is happening here, again. We're not getting involved in running those organizations. We're simply coming in with our skill sets. And what can be seen, of course, is that when you do this, the leverage is tremendous.

We had a very interesting meeting in New York recently with one of the state senators, a well-known individual and leader. He has been dean of social sciences at one of the universities, done a great deal of work in education, religion, tremendously aware of what's going on in the entire service sector—government entities, non-profits and the programs of religious institutions. One of the other people in attendance was a leader of the Orthodox Jewish School System. What was immediately apparent to the senator was that many of the same things we have done for the archdiocese could be applied right across the board for a wide range of school systems. In most cases, we probably have 70% of the work already done, with only small modifications required for the different entities. We can leverage directly on the previous contributions made—aiding these institutions by utilizing our skill sets to give them more time and resources to focus on the achievement of their missions and goals. The senator could see this tremendous opportunity for further contributions growing right out of the initial set of projects performed.

Let's just come back for a minute to Carl Jung, to one of his most often quoted statements, where he talks about all the patients he has treated over the years. "Among all patients in the second half of life—that is to say, over 35—it's safe to say that every one of them fell ill because they had lost that which the living religions of every age have given to their followers and none of them has really been healed who did not regain his religious outlook. This of course has nothing to do with a particular creed or membership in a church." A very powerful statement. This man doesn't say these people are ill because they didn't come see him or they didn't follow his methodology. He says, something quite different. And it seems to me he's saying, just as Kant says, there's a moral law that is there within us, and if people don't recognize it and hook into it, they're going to experience serious problems.

Again, trying to assess what's driving our people, let's look at Mother Teresa's Simple Path. Many of you may have seen this. My understanding is that a Muslim gentlemen was the first one who actually printed it. Of course Mother Teresa is known all over the world, but she says her life is guided by this Simple Path: the fruit of silence is prayer. She says she starts her prayers in silence so she can hear God speak to her. The fruit of prayer is faith. The fruit of faith is love. And it is the last two that I think are particularly important—the fruit of love is service, and the fruit of service is peace. People who meet her say Mother Teresa has an air of peace about her that is unrivalled. There is a peacefulness that she gets, and she is clear on its origin—it stems from her work. You look at this situation and you look at the response of our members to our activities and, even though our activities pale in comparison to the work Mother Teresa and her followers undertake, you can begin to sense the origin of the benefits which flow back to our members from properly balancing and integrating these activities into their working lives.

A close examination of these activities has revealed that another level of benefits exists relative to these types of activities and these benefits also flow in both directions. The work performed by the chapter member not only impacts the recipient organizations directly, it actually goes beyond that. The work also boosts the people that are running those organizations. Think about it for a minute. We're out on a mission, a tough job with limited resources and suddenly a group shows up and says they are here, they have some skills, and they would like to assist us in the achievement of our mission. We have got to feel good about that. And we can see exactly this quality of feeling in the comments of McCall, Bergin and Caputo as an example. In turn, these feelings, these sparks that are stimulated in the leaders of these organizations by the work of our members flow directly back to the members.

Another powerful example of the benefits flowing back to our members and their employees arose in connection with one of the state comptroller's projects that I did not review in detail with you. It was in connection with the accounting systems update project and the controller of one of our team members told a fascinating story. She said, when I selected my team to make the presentation at the joint meeting, those staff members chosen to be on the team were highly complimented that they had been picked to make the presentation. Furthermore, they were proud to be there to interact and share their knowledge. And she said they came back from the presentation feeling they had learned a tremendous amount . . . Think about what has happened there. The impact on these employees and, in turn, their organizations is both exciting and powerful. The controller provided the contrast when she said, in effect, "You know the funny thing is, that we are continually trying to present quality, in-house professional development programs but often these do not seem to go over very well. But I assign my employees to this type of project and they come back with an added degree of camaraderie, a new level of esprit de corps they've learned from the experience, and they're fired up regarding the continued performance of their jobs."

So you see the impact of these projects, again flowing directly back to these senior executives and their fellow employees, and clearly benefiting their organizations. It could almost be termed a reinvigoration process.

Right here, I must interject one other important fact that comes directly out of this work. That is, if our members with all of their work pressures and time constraints feel there's a need for these activities to be a part of our working lives, then what about the retired members of our society? Our chapter members' lives are so jammed and yet these members are still saying we have to do this work. There is a value associated with it. There is a reinvigoration that appears to be associated with it. And rather than individuals being drained as far as being able to do their actual jobs, they come back from these activities charged up, with an added zest for their work, and an increased respect for their organizations.

What about the retireds? What about the value of integrating a balanced amount of these activities into their lives? As our employees are moving toward retirement, we have opportunities to steer them in the directions of these activities, make them aware of the benefits they can bring to others and the benefits in turn they will experience—in other words—we can create the channels. And, of course that's what we've actually done, yet we didn't realize that at the outset. We created the channels, the channels by which our members, using their skill sets, could face off against some of the problems obstructing or hindering these various institutions in the achievement of their missions and goals.

When you think about the retireds that are out there, the potential is almost unlimited. At a time when many say we are faced with an ever-expanding morass of societal problems, we have these legions of retireds. Never before in the history of mankind has a country been blessed with such a pool of individuals who, for the most part, are healthy, intellectually capable and financially secure—who could face off against these societal problems. We, as senior financial executives and as members of senior management, may be able to play a critical role in building the bridges and cutting the channels that will allow this talented pool of retired citizens to move across and face off against these problems. What enormous progress could be made if these untapped resources could be matched up against the problems. And, if anyone can match these resources against the problems, we can do it because we do it all the time in our work. And does everyone win? It is clear—powerful wins are there for all involved.

Let me conclude at this point by asking that you carry with you the words of Margaret Mead that I think are particularly pertinent, relative to the opportunities that we have in front of us. I quote, "Never doubt that a small group of thoughtful, committed citizens can change the world. Indeed, it is the only thing that ever has."

APPENDIX II

Challenges Facing a Centrally Planned Economy: The Grace–Samuelson Exchange

The Quarterly Journal of Economics

May 1970

In the May 1970 issue of the Quarterly Journal of Economics (QJE), Paul Samuelson and one of the authors here, Stephen Grace, had an exchange regarding Samuelson's model contrasting the operation of a Free Enterprise economy with that of an economy operating under Efficient (Ideal) Planning.

Now, over fifty years later, that discussion of Samuelson's model seems to offer basic, important insights to certain issues being addressed currently by China, the U.S., and others regarding economic planning. Perhaps even more importantly, Samuelson and Grace identify and agree on serious impediments to the Chinese Efficient Planning approach.

The Samuelson-Grace discussion of the Efficient Planning Model and the Free Enterprise Model is reviewed in summary fashion here, omitting the complex mathematics set out in actual exchange. Operational considerations are then discussed.

I. The Model

Samuelson developed his original argument utilizing a spatial model where rival stores (or plants) locate on a circle along which customers are distributed evenly. One could imagine a volcanic island where everyone resided evenly around the perimeter. The farther goods must be transported, the greater the real costs. Over time, the number of store locations servicing the customers grows from one to eight.

Efficient Planning v. Free Enterprise

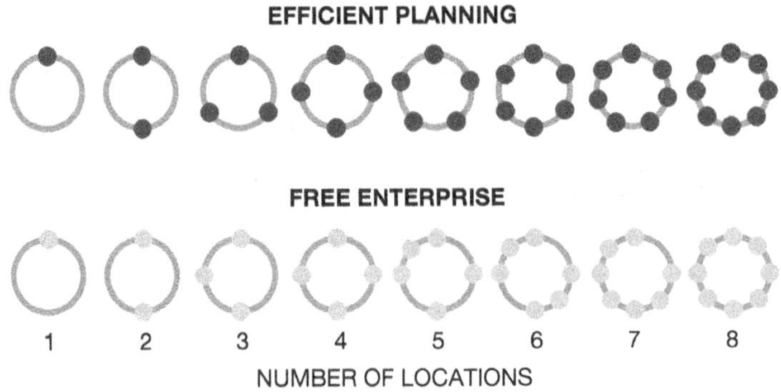

As the optimal number of stores moves from one to eight, the two rows of diagrams demonstrate the optimal arrangement for the stores under Efficient Planning and under Free Enterprise. When the optimal number of stores is one, the location of the one store is the same under both systems. Likewise, when the optimal number of stores is two. However, when the optimal number of stores increases to three, the arrangements under the two systems differ. At four stores, the locations are again identical, but at five, six, and seven stores the locations differ. At eight stores, the locations are the same under Free Enterprise and under Efficient Planning.

As Samuelson originally commented, the model appears to show improved locational arrangements under Efficient Planning in several cases relative to what is achieved under Free Enterprise. As the optimal number of stores moves from one to eight under Efficient Planning the respective store locations at each stage are properly arranged equidistant from the others. Yet in a number of cases the arrangement of the stores under Free Enterprise appears out of balance.

However, when one steps back and contrasts the two different methods, it becomes apparent that serious problems arise under Efficient Planning. The transition from two stores to three stores under Efficient Planning requires one of the two original stores be removed, and two new stores be put in place. Under Free Enterprise, no existing location is removed, only a single new store is put in place.

When the market grows to an optimal number of four stores, Efficient Planning requires two existing locations to be removed and three new locations to be put in place. The removal and development of five locations is required, while under Free Enterprise only the development of a single new location is required. When one stops to consider it, the differences in the efficiency of Efficient Planning and Free Enterprise are startling, with five economic decisions required to reach an optimal arrangement under Efficient Planning while only one economic decision is required under Free Enterprise.

The problems inside Efficient Planning do not stop there. In moving from three locations to four locations, the central authority controlling an efficient planning system must determine which stores will be removed and which owners impacted, where the new stores will be located, and who will develop and operate the three new stores. Such an arrangement provides the opportunity for the central authority not only to control the selection of those to be involved in the development and operation of the stores, but also to seek additional benefits personally and otherwise, including monetary and non-monetary compensation from those selected to operate ongoing control over the stores being retained or newly developed as well as those controlling the selected locations.

In contrast, the Free Enterprise economy, as it moves from two stores to three stores, motivates those involved in creating the third location to become more effective and efficient given that those controlling the new location will be faced with having a smaller market share than the two existing stores. Rather than controlling a third of the market, the new store will control one fourth (2/8's) of the marketplace while the two existing locations each control 3/8's of the marketplace. The fact that those controlling the new location provide their own financing only provides additional incentive for creativity and a push for optimal operations.

II. The Existence and Impact of Impediments

The history of political governance has shown that, while centralized authority structures such as monarchies and dictatorships appear streamlined and efficient in their decision-making, breakdowns inevitably occur in most. Any semblance of "tone at the top" is replaced by "personal preferences" and the absence of "checks and balances" leads to the failure to achieve optimal economic outcomes.

China, with a leader who has been designated to head the central authority until 2035, is following such a path, and appears at risk of experiencing less than optimal performance. The current restructuring of the government and governance of Hong Kong, and the restructuring of the manner in which China's private sector, both domestic and foreign owned, will operate with increased governmental involvement point to further tests for their Efficient Planning model as is demonstrated by the continuing collapses in the real estate market, and the Chinese government's decisions to encourage younger Chinese to migrate from the cities back to their villages.

The impact of the economic fundamentals Samuelson and Grace agreed on continue to loom large.

Index

A

Acton, Lord, 26, 42, 78–79
Archdiocese of New York School System, 77
Aristotle writings, 76, 79
Aurelius, Marcus, 24

B

Baruch College, 77
Bingle/SolarWinds, 10
board executive committee, 54–56
board governance, 27–28, 31–32
board management, 75, 77–81
  examining personal governance, 76–77
  gaps in financial information, 68
  internal reporting system, 72–73
  operation of company, 69
  responsibility, accountability and service, 77–80
  understanding and monitoring cash flows, 73
Boeing, 2, 3, 9–11, 13, 14, 30–32, 44, 50–52, 59, 61, 83, 86
Bowers, Reveta F., 83
Buffet, Warren, 67
Business Law Today (BLT), 32
Business Roundtable (BRT), 46–47

C

capital cash flows, 68–69
cash control, 69
cash flow management, 69
cash flow monitoring, 63–64
cash flow reporting structures, 72–73
cash flows, 67–74
  analytical model, 69–70
  authority for, 69
  board and, 67
  cash control activity, 70–71
  forecasting difficulties, 71–72
  gaps in financial information, 68–69
  liquidity requirements, 71–72
  reporting structures, 72–73
  tracking of, 68
Caremark test, 6–15
  Boeing decision, 9–11
  Marchand decision, 7–9
  McDonald's I, 11–13
  McDonald's II, 13–14
  Meta Platforms, 14–15
cash, 73
Chandler, William B., 30–32, 59, 81
checks and balances approach, 37–52
  board oversight and governance, 44–50
  director responsibilities, 50–52
  evolution to, 38–40
  focus from tone at top to, 40–42
  improving oversight and governance, 50
  oversight and governance, 44–50
  Volcker and Levitt on, 42–44
chief executive officer (CEO), 12, 15, 31, 37, 44–45, 47–48, 50–53, 55–56, 58, 67, 81–84
chief financial officer (CFO), 3–4, 22, 27–28, 48, 55–56, 65, 67–69, 71, 83
chief legal officer (CLO), 4, 48, 67–69, 71, 73
City University of New York (CUNY) system, 22, 77
corporate governance lawyer, 1–2, 4, 16, 30, 33, 37, 42, 44, 46–47, 50, 52, 56–58, 64, 67, 69, 74, 81, 86
corporate governance structure. *See* stress testing

D

democracy, 79
directors and officers (D&O), 8
Disney Case, 30
Disney, Roy E., 82

division of labor, 33
Dodd-Frank Act, 64

E
earnings management, 38–39
Easterbrook, Stephen J., 12
economic well-being vs financial well-being, 76
Eisner, Michael, 52, 82–83
executive committee, 55–56. *See also* board executive committee

F
Fairhurst, David, 12
Financial Executives International (FEI), 21, 77, 79
Fogel, Robert, 20–23, 49, 76–78

G
general counsel (GC), 67
generally accepted accounting principles (GAAP), 68
governance structures
  stress testing, 29–30
  under the microscope, 33–36

H
Hunter College, 77

I
intellectual capital, 75–77. *See also* board management; personal governance systems
Isaiah writings, 18–19, 76

J
Jung, Carl, 19

K
Kennedy, John F., 79

L
Laster, J. Travis, 11
Levitt, Arthur, 38–43
Lincoln, Abraham, 79
Luther King, Jr., Martin, 79

M
material information, 65
Miller, Ron W., 82

N
Neuhaus, Rev. Richard John, 25–26
New York City (NYC) Chapter, 21, 77
non-monetary compensation, 75

O
O'Donovan, Leo J., 83
Office of the State Comptroller, 77
operational cash flows, 68–70
organizational governance, 1, 18, 25–27, 37, 79, 85
  board interaction, 82–84
  board members, 16–18, 81–82
  Caremark duties, 6–16
  cash flow monitoring, 63–64
  checks and balances approach, 37–52
  economics of, 5–6
  evolution of, 67
  information gaps, 60–62
  internal information, 59–60
  internal reporting, 63
  non-GAAP measures in external reporting, 62–63
Ovid, Roman poet, 78–79
Ovitz, Michael, 83

P
personal governance system, 1, 4, 18–23, 76–77
Poitier, Sidney, 83
political governance, 1, 18, 23–25, 29, 42, 78, 103
Public Interest Initiatives Committee (PIIC), 21

Q
Quarterly Journal of Economics (QJE), 23–24

R
red flags, 12
role in litigation, 32
Russell, Irwin, 83

S
Samuelson, 24
Sarbanes-Oxley Act, 64
Smith, Adam, 23
stress testing, 29–36

T
Tao Te Ching writings, 76, 79
The Wall Street Journal, 42
toolmakers, 20–21, 76

U
U.S. Government C.F.O.'s Council, 77
United Nations Institute for Training and Research (UNITAR), 77

V
Veasey, Norman E., 31–32, 45, 58, 81
Volcker, Paul, 42–43

W
Walt Disney, 30, 52, 82–83
Washington, George, 79
Wells Fargo, 2, 30–31, 44–45, 56, 81–83
Wells, Frank, 82–83
Wilson, Gary, 83

Y
Y State Public Employees' Retirement System (YPERS), 33–36

About the Authors

H. Stephen Grace, Jr., Ph.D.

Stephen has been addressing organization governance issues for over 50 years going back to his May 1970 exchange with Nobel Economist Paul Samuelson in *The Quarterly Journal of Economics* ("Professor Samuelson on Free Enterprise and Economic Influence: A Comment"). As founder and president of H.S. Grace & Company, Inc. ("HSG"), he has been involved in a broad range of consulting assignments and has been retained as a testifying expert in over 150 matters. His work has focused on complex business issues including organization governance and business conduct.

Previously, he served as National Director at Large with Touche Ross &Co./ Deloitte & Touche, President and CEO of Dane Development Corporation; Vice President of Finance and CFO of Century Corporation; and simultaneously served as Senior Vice President and CFO of Century Development Corporation; and Assistant Treasurer of Zapata Corporation.

His professional and community affiliations include: Financial Executives International - national chairman 2003-2004, member of the office of the chairman, president of the New York City and Houston chapters, area director, area vice president, and trustee of The Financial Executives Research Foundation and member of Committee on Governance, Risk and Compliance; Forbes CFO Forum Advisory Board; New York State Society of CPAs (NYSSCPA) - Quality Enhancement Policy Committee (advisor); Lamar University College of Engineering - Advisory Council - founding member; Lamar University College of Business - Advisory Council; Jesse H. Jones School of Business, Texas Southern University - Advisory Council; Calvert House, University of Chicago - Advisory Council.

His library of publications and addresses is set out on the HSG website. Articles prior to the creation of the HSG website are available.

Suzanne H. Gilbert

Suzanne spent 30 years within the Interpublic Group of Companies (IPG). She retired as Vice Chair-WW CFO at Initiative Media. Prior to that she was WW-CFO at Lowe Lintas & Partners Worldwide, EVP-Chief Financial & Administrative Officer at Campbell-Ewald Worldwide, and SVP-Finance & Administration at Clinton E. Frank Advertising.

She currently is a member of the board of advisors of Grace & Co. Consultancy, Inc. and for the previous nine years was on the board of directors of a private electric vehicle company where she chaired its audit committee and sat on the compensation, corporate governance, and transactions committees. She is active in Financial Executives International and its national committee on governance, risk and compliance, and previously served as president of its Detroit chapter. She is an elected member of the International Women's Forum and past treasurer of its Chicago Forum.

Previously, she served on the board of trustees of Fielding Graduate University and chaired its finance, investment, and IT committees; the Detroit Workforce Development Commission executive board; the American Association of Advertising Agencies (AAAA) insurance company board and its investment and audit committees; as well as local civic board associations.

She received her MBA from the University of Chicago-Booth School of Business and a BS from Marquette University, where at each school she was a member of Beta Gamma Sigma.

Joseph P. Monteleone, Esq.

Joe has over 40 years of industry experience, including 25 as a claims professional and executive. Through his firm, Catamount Services LLC, he offers consulting and other services to policyholders, insurance companies, brokers, and others. As an arbitrator and mediator, he specializes in disputes involving insurance coverage issues. His expert witness services include testimony on insurance industry custom and practice, as well as claims handling standards. His consulting services include policy and endorsement drafting and reinsurance audits.

His specialty areas of expertise are management liability insurance products, such as directors and officers, and other complex professional liability and errors and omissions coverages, including but not limited to transactional risk insurance, lawyers professional, and employment practices liability. He has been a frequent speaker and writer during his extensive professional career, including publications and presentations in the United States, Europe, and Asia.

Joe is a certified arbitrator through ARIAS-US, a CPR-trained mediator, and is admitted to practice of law in New York and New Jersey. He is currently a member of the board of advisors at Grace & Co. Consultancy, Inc.

S. Lawrence Prendergast

Larry earned a degree in mathematics from Brown University and an MBA from NYU. He served as VP and Treasurer of AT&T, as well as CEO and Chair of AT&T Investment Management Corp. He also served as EVP of LaBranche & Co., a NYSE firm.

Larry is currently Chair of the Turrell Fund and serves on private equity boards at JP Morgan. He has served on four public company boards and is the author of the book *Uncommon Profits Through Stock Purchase Warrants* published by Dow-Jones Irwin. He currently is a member of the Board of Advisors of Grace & Co. Consultancy, Inc.